Wrangling Squirrels

Project management lessons you won't learn in school

By
Kasun Gamage, PMP, PMI-ACP
Dan Strandt
EJ Ellis

"… Furnished with well researched perspectives, it can be easy to lose track of time caught into project management insights, does and donts and other tricks. The result is a view of the world which is encouraging and hopeful. All having the right mindset. If you're looking for some inspiration that reshapes change management, you have high chances to find it." -A. Rus, PMP

"… Clear, concise & easy to understand examples will help anyone understand the basic principles behind the concept of project management." - S. Bose, PMP

"…gives you a guidance how you can manage your relationship with your manager and make life easier for you and your team. The writer uses storytelling in order to make the content of the chapter more interesting and understandable to readers." L. Kafkas, PMP

Contents

CHAPTER 1 INTRODUCTION 1
CHAPTER 2 SELECTING THE RIGHT TEAM 4
CHAPTER 3 MANAGING UP 24
CHAPTER 4 RESPONDING TO CHANGE 43
CHAPTER 5 NEGOTIATING 57
CHAPTER 6 DELEGATING 77
CHAPTER 7 FIRING SOMEONE 96
CHAPTER 8 CONFLICT MANAGEMENT 114
CHAPTER 9 MANAGING SCOPE 129
CHAPTER 10 MEASURING PROGRESS, SUCCESS, AND FAILURE 141
CHAPTER 11 GOALS 154

CHAPTER 1 INTRODUCTION

"Management is, above all, a practice where art, science, and craft meet."
-Henry Mintzberg

The squirrel: bushy-tailed bully or savvy scavenger? Rascally rodent or curious climber? From sprawling grasslands to urban jungles, the squirrel is among the most visible of our wildlife, but despite their fluffy features, we're often undecided—friend or foe?

Incredibly quick on their feet and able to run up and down trees at impressive speeds, their physicality alone should lend itself to make them more likable. They're smart as well. Smart enough to navigate themselves through obstacles; to find the most efficient shortcuts to the food they've buried, or to escape airborne predators. Why then are we still undecided?

As a project manager, you will face similar dichotomy. Perhaps not birdseed and power line mischief, but a lack of direction and leadership can propagate the same type of frenzied working environment we equate with our furry foe's lifestyle. A good project manager must maintain a strong working relationship with their team, channeling their best attributes towards a singular goal; think of it as wrangling squirrels.

Let's imagine you have six squirrels running around your office, working on a project managed by you. Each goes about their daily rituals and duties; they're climbing up and down cubicle walls in a rush, prowling conference rooms to get a message across, snooping around in the hallways to find a stakeholder. To someone outside of the project it might appear to be a scene lacking direction and purpose, complete chaos; but you know better.

The squirrel analogy can represent your project team and stakeholders, a group of different people each focused on different tasks, scrambling around in different directions, each going about their duties. Or for you, the squirrel might represent your senior managers and other department heads—different leads with different expertise, all trying to give enough attention to your project, but they are pressed for time and resources. The squirrels could also be your suppliers, vendors, other external partners, and third-party collaborators—groups with different motives, each typically difficult to negotiate with. The analogy even works for the resources in your project such as costs and timelines— constantly changing, regardless of your best efforts to apply for some order. As a project manager, your job is to wrangle these squirrels by providing direction and purpose. However, it is easier said than done.

Circumstances arise and overthrow your initial plans. Conflicts arise, and people become irrational and emotional. Your stakeholders might change their minds mid-project. Your funding might get cut without warning. Everything is going well and then one small change throws the entire project into a completely different direction.

There are limited patterns of success. Being an efficient project manager begins with efficient planning. Remember, while some things may be unavoidable, it's not to say that they're unmanageable. A detailed, calculated and achievable plan is the foundation of any successful project: Set SMART goals, oversee your team's (and your own) timeline, understand different operation models and systems, and be open to the possibility of all the above changing during the project's lifetime.

Many academic institutions offer courses and classes on the skills necessary for project management. Make the most out of them. Undergoing formal training will sharpen your hard skills and provide you with grounding in the world of project management. However, don't expect more than that—a grounding. A complete, well-rounded lead player in a project has a set of strong soft skills in addition to an academic understanding: communication, interpersonal intelligence, negotiation, and delegation. These are neither easily teachable, nor formulaic; there is no fixed model of success. Hands-on experience is required to fully understand and master these skills. Knowledge is most effective when applied and practiced. Every project that you begin, tackle and end is the academia for learning these skills. With some hands-on practice, your efforts and investment in building effective project management skills will pay off. Immerse yourself in many projects; each will be unique and will bring with it new experiences.

As a project manager, you will be in a position that requires you to constantly interact with people—your team, your senior managers, your clients, and your customers. Project management goes beyond the study of business and operations; it also has more than a touch of social science and psychology. Understanding how people think, what motivates them, how they perceive situations, what their attitudes are towards you and the job is all valuable information in planning your management strategies.

In this book, we will explore many important concepts that have been overlooked in the contemporary teaching of project management. The text is heavily scenario-based, focused on real-life situations that we, as project managers, have experienced during countless project life cycles.

CHAPTER 2 SELECTING THE RIGHT TEAM

"Talent wins games, but teamwork and intelligence win championships."
-*Michael Jordan*

The success of any project relies heavily on all the people who collaborate to make it happen. Project management is not a one-man operation; it takes the collective efforts of a group of people working towards one common goal. Ideally, you will want to include the following characteristics in your team: stable, role-defined, responsible, and aligned with your goals and strategies. You want your team to have a clear understanding of the objectives and the goals so that they can engage, take responsibility and own decisions that will affect the project. The right team is motivated, committed, and empowered.

Now, the big question here is, how does a project manager build his team?

The traditional approach to project management teaches us to follow the classic method of selecting team members. This may include consulting with peers, possibly with Human Resource Departments, using RACI charts, and other strategies that can help a project manager identify which people are the best fit. However, the real quick is: should you hire the best candidate or the right candidate?

Choosing the right people

You would think you have to be working with the best, and this initially makes sense when working on a project. The traditional method of hiring your team usually results in hiring the team with certain skills, the most qualified individuals. However, choosing the *right* people to collaborate with is even more critical. A perfectly round puzzle piece is probably not going to fit; that oddly shaped one next to it may be exactly what you need. Wrangling squirrels is already tough enough, but it isn't as difficult to manage project teams when you have the right people on board.

First things first, every project needs to begin with a project plan. This project plan will include a resource plan for the project team. The resource plan will tell us the necessary project roles, responsibilities, reporting relationships, and other expectations for the project team. Setting clear job roles and responsibilities will save you the trouble of your team getting confused with their tasks and deliverables and encountering potential conflict or un-constructive disagreements. Project team roles must be clear, compatible, complementary, complete, and comprehensive. This plan identifies what is expected from each project team member, so they can function with minimal supervision and can follow through with their specific assignments. We have identified some high-quality resource plan templates to make this first step easier for you. You can find them at: www.wranglingsquirrels.com/resources

A well-developed project plan will also tell us the limits and scopes of the team members in relation to the project itself, including the extent of participation and influence each person will have. This will help the project team members develop effective and efficient processes. The resource plan will also include the chain of command that breaks down the reporting relationships in the project teams, meaning who reports to whom.

Before recruiting team members, make sure to outline each job title with their respective description and specifications. This will be helpful in the next step of identifying the right people for your project team—that is the staff acquisition.

In staff acquisition, the common-sense approach tells us to base our project team decisions on functionality. Basically, we're taught to look at the KSA's: knowledge, skills, and abilities. The functionality will tell us if the person is the right fit for the role itself. You wouldn't hire an accountant to do the job of a physicist, right? Maybe. The user's experience and competence are crucial in this aspect of selection; however, this is where the job description and specifications come into play. When picking the best players for your team, you must consider previous experience, competencies, skills, personality, character, and personal interests. All these factors must be considered and matched with the specifications of the job. Ideally, the person who best fits the role will have a profile that corresponds strongly to the requirements and expectations of the job. This is a very critical process because, at this point, you need to be 100% objective with your choices. It's important you keep objectivity in mind as you continue through this chapter.

The selection process does not end with this technique. On the surface, this practical approach appears to be the clear-cut method in forming project teams. However, having the most appropriate and best potential talent on board does not ensure the success of a project. An additional approach is being widely recognized by organizations where they acknowledge that having the best functional experts may not always lead to the best performance within the confines of a specific project.

As we have previously emphasized, the success of the project relies heavily on the people who will be working on it. Therefore, it is crucial that you hire not only the best fit for the role but the right *kind* of people for your project.

Before we go into more detail on the selection process, lets illustrate this concept with a practical, real-life scenario. Consider this story about Mike Williams of Gatley & Wright and how he discovered the value of recruiting the correct team members the hard way.

Nobody at the offices of Gatley & Wright Traders was more excited about this year's work Christmas Party than long-serving sales rep Mike Williams. Every December a different area of business is placed in charge of the planning and overseeing the festive hi-jinx. This year it was the Sales team, and after a group vote, Mike had landed the prestigious role of 'Santa Claus', an informal term given to the nominated project manager—the Father of the Christmas party. Now anybody familiar with work Christmas parties know that they often come with more baggage than the Kardashian family private jet but do it right, and the evening's merry antics and intoxicated faux pas' will be remembered forever in office folklore. The resounding success of the 09' party, hosted by the legends of the Marketing department, earned that year's Santa Claus a promotion from company director Steve Wright. Ever since there has been a pleasant Christmas bonus awarded to the man leading the sleigh. What ensued was a fierce inter-office rivalry, each department desperate to one-up the party of the year before. So, with great excitement, Mike gathered his team of little helpers into the office boardroom, all of them eager to hear the plans for what was going to be the Christmas party to end all Christmas parties.

The members of Sales were stuffed in the boardroom as tightly as the breadcrumbs you would find in the cavity of a Christmas Day poultry. "Who here knows the meaning of Christmas?" Mike asked his team from the head of the table. "The Birth of Santa," Janice confidently replied. Mike shook his head, saying: "I'm talking about the true meaning of Christmas." There was a ponderous silence before Rich chimed in: "To give to others? Bring happiness and joy to everyone around you?"

Mike started to rise from his chair, proclaiming: "The true meaning of Christmas is to deliver one night of the year that everybody in this office will never forget. Well, a night that they'll never forget and never remember." He walked over to the whiteboard and wrote down 'XMAS' in big letters. "XMAS: Excessive Marketing and Singing." A few colleagues turned to each other with raised eyebrows. "I want this to be the most talked about Christmas Party in Gatley & Wright history. I want people singing to the rooftops about its inevitable brilliance. I want every worker in this office sleepless the night before, eagerly awaiting me, Father Christmas, to deliver them the best gift of their working year." Rich raised his hand, claiming: "That's basically what I said, right?"

"Your intentions were good," Mike replied, "Now, I can't do this by myself. This will require a team effort. That's where you guys come in." Mike took to the whiteboard and compiled a list of tasks that would need seeing to. "How do you think Santa Claus delivers presents to millions of homes, across seven different continents, all in one night? I'll give you a clue, it's two words." Janice promptly pipes up again - "Christmas Miracle?" Mike shakes his head, replying: "A little thing I like to call project management." There were even more raised eyebrows across the room now. "I've been given a rather juicy five-figure budget from head office and have taken the time to break that down across five important areas. You'll be paired up and each assigned a category."

Mike pulled a folded piece of paper from his pocket and began dividing out the roles. "Sarah and Chris, you'll be in charge of sourcing the venue. I'm thinking a large function room, big tables, lots of space for games, somewhere classy. Mike and Sharon, you'll be looking after decorations, I want the room looking like Santa's grotto on steroids: bigger, louder, sparklier than we've ever seen before." People were jotting down their instructions." Janice and Rich, you'll be ordering the food and organizing the games. I want a spread big enough to fill old Saint Nick's plump belly AND his Reindeer's' greedy chops. Danny and Beth, you're in charge of sending out the invites and sorting out transportation to and from the office, make people feel like they're on the guest list for Santa's very own house party and make sure there are cabs for them by the time they stumble out with goodness know who."

There was a buzz around the room as the pairings dreamt up their wildest Christmas fantasies, everybody most esteemed of name and title would be talking about this for years to come. "Mick and Becca I'm leaving you to sort the music, put together a playlist that would have Santa twerking on his candy cane. Keep me updated with any bookings you make, CC me in emails, get me in on calls. Apart from that, anything goes," Mike said with a face that looked like it had been slapped by a palm full of confidence. "That leaves me with only one position left to assign." The whole of the room turned their attention to young George Wright sitting quietly at the back of the room.

George Wright was the son of Steve Wright, co-founder, and director of Gatley & Wright Traders. And kinship aside, there was little to justify George's position as a trusted member of staff at Gatley & Wright Traders. A nice lad, but slower than the office computer still running Windows XP. George had been lumped in the team as a "Thanker," a role created especially for him. His 'Job' was to make follow-up calls to clients that had already signed deals, thank them for their business, and tell them if there's anything they needed that they shouldn't hesitate to get in touch: basically a ploy to keep his involvement with anything important down to a minimum, whilst still making the boss feel as though his son was an 'asset' to the family business.

Mike cleared his throat. "George, I'm giving you the most important role there is. You're going to be my deputy. My second in command." This was the biggest eyebrow-raiser of the day. "You're going to be my eyes and ears. I don't want you to leave my shadow whenever we're working on this." Mike decided on this course of action because it meant that George would have no direct involvement in any of the important organization. However, there was a risk that with the inept, cocky lad at his side there may be a chance that George would put his foot in it around one of the business partners Mike dealt with. This was a risk that Mike deemed justified since, and this was what decided it for him, it meant that little George would tell Daddy that he played a key part in the success of the best Christmas party in the company's history, inevitably earning Mike even more brownie points than he'd already been collecting. "I won't let you down, boss," cried George from the back of the room.

Over the course of the next month, the plans came together better than Mother's Christmas pudding mix. Everything was in place; the dream was about to become a reality. True to Mike's command, "Excessive Marketing and Singing," there had been more talk about tomorrow's Christmas party than the kiss Rich and Janice had been caught sharing in the coffee room a few weeks back - a constant source of gossip at lunchtimes.

The event was being hosted at the Fenway Hotel and Spa, located just on the outside of town. With only twenty-four hours until party time, Mike was taking the day to head down to the place for some final checks on the function room. In his shadow was George, still fresh from doing a grand total of nothing to contribute to the project. Just as Mike had hoped. The pair were met at the reception desk and greeted by Laura, the Hotel manager. "I think you're going to be very happy with how it has all come together," she promised.

Laura began showing them around the function room. Mike ticked off on his clipboard as they went along, noting all the requested services were to the expected high-quality. As the due date was now imminent Mike was beginning to feel the strain of stress, but Laura's calm demeanor and reassuring the conversation eased his anxieties. Unfortunately, for Mike, George seemed less interested in the numbers that could fit in the function room, and more interested in fitting Laura's number in his phone book. She deflected with mature professionalism, but George was still uninterested in the purposes of the function room save, that is, for the gigantic 72-inch LCD screen on the wall, repeatedly asking how to turn it on whilst pressing at buttons on the side.

Laura was getting visibly frustrated as she pointed out it was new and hadn't been set up yet, but even then, it was for wedding events only. Eventually, she questioned whether they were taking the booking seriously since this was their most profitable night of the year and they had to have a reliable customer. She spoke regretfully of a mishap at last year's Christmas party, where an intoxicated estate agent burst into the room wearing an entire raw turkey on his head, yelling 'Gobble Gobble!' every time he bumped into a wall or tripped over a table. The entire room had to be shut for 48 hours whilst it was scoured clean of any lingering bacteria.

Mike took action to get George out of the picture, handing him two sheets of paper and pointing him towards the bar, asking him to get a list of prices so they could work out how many free drinks they could assign to each staff member. George sauntered away as Mike was ushered off for a tour of the reception area, cloakroom, and car park. When Mike got back to ask George for the report, he noticed not only were the two sheets blank, but George himself was three sheets to the wind after taking a more hands-on approach to discovering the range on sale. Mike stopped in his tracks. "You're more loaded than a rich kid's Christmas stocking! You heard Laura, we must be seen as a reliable customer. This has to go off without a hitch or we're both going to be in big trouble!" George slurred "Pfft, chill out Mike. I'm the director's son. Like anything's gonna' happen to me. Relax a little - here, try the eggnog, it's deliciously creamy and strong as a mule's kick." At that moment, Laura appeared behind Mike and, panicking, he hastily pushed George away. He turned to her and said: "Well, everything seems fine here. We'll just be off now; you have my number if you need…"

Suddenly there was the sound of an enormous crash behind him, and with a frozen heart, he turned. He was met with the sight of George extricating himself from underneath the LCD screen, or more accurately, the heap of frayed wires and snapped plastic that was left of it. Upon meeting Mike's traumatized gaze George mumbled: "Barely even touched it, boss," then drank from his eggnog, swallowing a screw in the process.

Laura snatched the clipboard out of George's hand, declaring: "The party's off! We'll be sending your company the bill this afternoon," before walking away, finishing as she got to the door with "and a Merry Christmas to you too!"

The next evening Mike sat at home in his underwear and read again the company e-mail that announced the cancellation and subsequent disbandment of the team, and his eyes lingered on the final sentence - "Unfortunately Santa crashed the sleigh. No presents this year! I know who's getting coal for Christmas…," signed – George Wright.

The easiest way to remember the most critical aspects of team member selection is with a new set of acronyms – the 3W's: The Want, the Way, and the Will. The right employees don't just make the cut–they also have the right fit with their passion, their abilities, and their capacities.

The WANT

The Want tells you about the motives of the person and to what extent they will be committed to the project and the team. This is where you assess their passion.

Ask yourself: Between an enthusiastic but less experienced candidate and a burnt-out expert, who would you rather have on your team?

Motivation and passion matter when identifying the right people to join your team. You want to know why a candidate wants to participate in a project and how badly the candidate wants it.

Here is another good point to ponder on: A self-serving individual will seek what he can get from a project; a servant-leader will seek what he can give to a project. The right people will have the best interest of the project in mind, their motives will be genuine. Their purpose will be bigger than the tasks that will be assigned to them and the position they hold. The right people are passionate about their project and their work. They have an aligned sense of purpose and find pleasure in doing what they do. Passionate workers are motivated and satisfied workers. When you have the right people working, you won't have to question their motivations and you can trust they have the right interest in pursuing the project because they are passionate about it. You would know that they actually want to be there and that they can commit to the role that will be assigned to them.

So, how do you assess their passion and motivation?

Here is one of the situations where your resource plan will be very useful. To assess a candidate's motives and desire for a project, it's important to first clearly define what will be expected of them in relation to their role in the project team. Before agreeing on anything, present to them the role description. Explain the project rationale, objectives, the position, expectations, work environment, and all the other aspect of being a part of the project team. Afterward, ask them directly what they think about the responsibility, ask them if they are challenged or motivated. Knowing how they perceive the project and the position will give you an idea about the level of commitment the person can give to the project.

Upon discussing the objective of the project, you must ensure that the candidate has a clear and comprehensive understanding of the team's common goal... There are some individuals who would jump into your journey just to catch a free ride and enjoy the perks of your project. Let's call these people the free-riders. Free-riders are people who have the wrong kind of motivation to join a team. For them, if they feel they will be receiving the same kind of benefits without participating or playing their part, they won't pull their weight. Having a free-rider in your team will not only be a problem for you as the project leader, but his presence can also be detrimental to the morale and performance to everyone else in the group. Free riders can sometimes be identified as social loafers. In the study of psychology, social loafing is the tendency of individuals to exert less effort when they are working in a group than they would individually. This can create undesirable group dynamics and decreased performance and efficiency among your team.

Let's illustrate this with a very brief example. A project team of ten members has been working tirelessly to meet one of their deadliest deadlines. One team member, let's call him Fred, suddenly calls in to inform the team that he won't be able to show and help because of a "prior commitment." The rest of the team members then worked together to fill in his absence. On the day of the presentation, Fred shows up and stands with everyone else, taking credit for the collective effort of the team. In this scenario, you would understand why the rest of the team members may feel frustrated and even lose motivation. In some cases, team members with confronting personalities might even clash with the free-riders and cause unhealthy conflicts within the group.

Understanding a candidate's WANT to be part of the project team is of vital importance. As discussed, hiring a person whose motives are not aligned with the project objectives and whose commitment does not match the rest of the team's poses a threat. A threat that can hinder you and your team from achieving your goals.

Motivated team members are more productive and are more able to deliver better input. They are more satisfied with their roles and responsibilities. They are committed to achieving higher levels of performance and commit to going the extra mile. Project team members who are passionate about their roles are on the constant prowl to improve. To them, no problem is difficult enough to keep them away from succeeding.

At this point, let us go back to the earlier question: Between an enthusiastic but less experienced candidate and a burnt-out expert, whom would you rather have on your team? Remember, competence and mastery should not be your sole qualifier in determining if a person will be the right fit for your team. Check his motives, his commitment, his passion – these are the elements that will truly define his WANTS.

The WAY

The Way is the project team member's ability to function in the team with the role that is assigned to him. In addition, when speaking about functionality, we don't just talk about titles and certifications.

When selecting project team members, look for skills, knowledge, and experience over titles. Look beyond the certifications and evaluate if the person is capable of delivering and being productive. Determine the soft skills of the candidate. This can be done through a thorough screening process with research, interviews, and assessments. Ask about their professional background; ask about their passions, about the steps they have taken to get to where they are today. This is essential because past behaviors are often great indicators of future behavior. You would want to have a glimpse of the WAYS a candidate will carry out his role and function.

When selecting people, we don't just look at what they can do, but also HOW they do things. It doesn't take much to know that working is easier with positive personalities than with the negative. Pessimists will always have a problem for every solution, wherein optimists will seek to find a solution to every problem. You also want to be on the lookout for integrity. Simply put, integrity is doing the right thing when nobody is watching. Ideally, project teams are trustworthy, reliable, and accountable. Look for people who will embrace the project and take full responsibility for their tasks. You can trust these people because people with integrity are likely to be self-disciplined and proactive. Employees who are responsible enough to act on their own are valuable assets to any project.

Another approach to assess their WAYS is to gauge their emotional strength. When working on a project in a team, you will often face situations where you may be criticized or faced with conflicts or even fail. The ability to manage one's personal emotions, to take the good with the bad, and to accept and adapt any situation no matter how challenging, are skills critical for a successful project. You can assess a person's emotional strength by observing how they respond to and behave in difficult situations, such as when they are stressed, or in disagreement with colleagues. A project team player must be mentally and emotionally strong. Projects are often not without risk. There are situations where a project may encounter setbacks, or worst-case scenario, may even fail and need to be withdrawn. You want to have people in your team who can be objective and responsible enough to own up to their decisions.

In determining their personal WAYS and approach to work, you want to have a good mix of personalities in your team. Tradition is nice, but it gets old. When aiming for dynamic and innovative success, you want different kinds of ideas and input. A fresh perspective could be what you need. It will be helpful to look for people who are not only results-oriented but also creative and visionary. Don't be afraid to look for people who don't share the exact same characteristics as you–remember, there is strength in diversity. The trick is to find the right kind of variety for your team.

Our brains are wired in a way that it unconsciously creates a bias that favors people who are like ourselves. The brain focuses on what's familiar to it, and the most familiar to us is ourselves. In evaluating potential candidates, this tendency leads our brains to have a subjective favor for those who are like us. Now, you must be cautious about this. As mentioned, it's important to be 100% objective in selecting your project team members. When putting together your project team, you want to find ways to incorporate diverse outlooks and background. Having a group of different-minded people in your team will give you the advantages of identifying risks better and finding more creative solutions. In addition, the more diverse your project team is, the more client population your team can represent.

So, how can you create a diverse project team?

It can be a good idea to mix the demographics in your team, so team members can have something different to bring to the table. Consider getting a good gender balance of male and female representatives. Age can also be telling of the experiences a team member might have; try to get the right balance of individuals from different age groups. If you want to aim for a globally competitive team, it might be helpful to ensure that you have a diverse mix of nationalities in your team. This not only opens your project to a variety of ideas and input from different cultures and background, but it also gives you a multi-national representation that can widen your target client population.

Executing projects may require you to have broad networks and strong influences in the company. For this, you might need to look for resourceful and influential individuals who have professional connections with different organizations and individuals both inside and outside the company. The connector type of member will have the WAYS to know whom to reach out to and how to get things done in case your project hits a bump along the road.

You will also want to keep an eye out for people who are both teachers and learners, who are happy to rotate in the coaching cycle. It is not uncommon in projects for every project team member to take turns in being both a mentor and a mentee.

Effective communication remains to be the number one key to the success of any project. It will help you to get team members who are great communicators. They will know how to listen, how to talk, and how to respect others. This is important especially in times of conflict. When the project hits a bump, you need people who will have the WAYS to discuss the issues within your group, not avoid them defensively.

And speaking of group dynamics, it pays to observe the WAYS on how candidates interact with other people–people whom they work with, whom they work for, and who work for them. As you observe them, try to assess how they value and interact with people, especially people who are "beneath" them. This is an effective way to tell a person's character and if they have the potential to become compassionate and influential leaders. It will also help you tell how the person will blend within a team.

While it is essential that the person has the WAYS to fit in the job role, it's just as important that the person also has the WAYS to fit in with the rest of the team. Project managers should consider how compatible the individual is with the personalities of the team members and the organization itself, and how committed he will be to the project. Here, we look at personality, motivations, and values–how are these aligned with the project objectives? Shared values are non-negotiable. Although it's important to find people capable of independent thinking and bringing new and different ideas to the table, it's more vital to ensure that you find the right team players who understand the values of your organization and the direction of your project, who share these principles, and who can commit themselves to the team.

For the best people to be the right people, they have to have the right WAYS to function in the team. Project teams need to have effective processes that are well defined, documented, uncomplicated, and stable. It not only paves the way to get things done but the way to work unitedly and interdependently as well.

At this point, your resource plan once again comes in handy. Project team members know that a house needs to be built, but, more importantly, they need to know the specifics: How many floors? How many rooms? How wide is the area? Will it have a backyard? An indoor pool? Project team members need to be able to understand the objectives, and to have a shared goal. A clear end goal paves the WAY for every decision and action in the project.

The WILL

Will is the person's capacity to carry out his role and responsibilities. You will need team members who won't be just committed and able, but also have the actual time and resources to deliver – in short, is available and can say he WILL get the job done. It would be difficult to expect somebody who is already loaded with a different job to carry on another role in your team. Although it might have the skill and the interest and might seem to be the best fit, his incapacity to be a team player will not make him the right person.

On top of their KSAs, project managers should also look at the individual's satisfaction, engagement, and commitment. These leadership attributes have been linked with higher performance and better group dynamics where team players go the extra mile and cultivate a positive atmosphere in the group. For projects to be launched successfully and to continuously grow, you need people who are willing to be committed to their work even at times of risk, setbacks, boredom, conflict, and other negative situations.

You also want to ensure that your team members will commit not only to specific individuals but to the team as a whole. It also matters how the candidate will fit along with the rest of the team. Highly cohesive teams tend to be more successful and perform better. Teamwork is a mean to the end goal. Take a look at their personalities and see how they blend in with everyone else. Immerse your team in activities that can strengthen their interpersonal work relationships for a better social atmosphere. Babe Ruth once said, "The way a team plays as a whole determines its success. You may have the greatest bunch of individual stars in the world, but if they don't play together, the club won't be worth a dime." Even if you find the best individuals who are the right fit for the roles you need for your project, if they don't play or ride along well together, you won't be able to get anywhere. It will help you find team members who will be able to take pride and enjoy working with your team.

Consider how much energy a candidate can exert for the project. You want to be on the lookout for energetic individuals who are buzzing with life and vitality; those who are eager to learn and get their hands dirty. When faced with the option to choose between a candidate who has years of experience but shows signs of burnout and weariness and a candidate who is fresh from university, lacks a strong working background but is radiating with the potential to commit and deliver, whom would you rather have on your team? When talking about capacities, this includes not just their time and will, but also their energy and enthusiasm to take on the role. This goes hand in hand with their motives and commitment.

So, how can you assess a person's WILL and capacity to function in your team?

Again, we resort to your project resource plan. Based on the information you have gathered on the candidate about his competence, skills, experiences, motivations, passions, and other hard and soft skills, evaluate the expected workload and his personal and professional attributes. Does the candidate have the energy to take on the role? Will he be able to give and commit his time and resources to the project? Will he be loyal to the team and the project goals?

Some people might look highly qualified. However, you should review how much time they will be able to commit to the project. It may cause you some trouble to get someone who is already juggling multiple responsibilities in the organization. While the person may be highly competent and has all the necessary skills for a role in the team, if he can't commit to attending regular meetings, or answer immediately to urgent concerns or show up in project-related activities, it will end doing more harm than good. You might end up having to tap others to fill in his task, or maybe even do them yourself.

On that note, it pays to seek out people that have organizational and time management skills. You want people who show up to every meeting and submit their deliverables on time. Deadlines are crucial matters in projects. And because highly effective teams work interdependently, having one person who fails to meet the timelines can slow everyone down and delay the entire project. The right kind of people will also have the will to identify problem areas and resolve issues in a timely manner. They are matured enough to manage conflict in a professional and constructive manner.

Willful team players are among the best kind. They have initiative and are self-directed and proactive. These are people who can work under minimal supervision and act on their own. As a project manager, you can trust willful team players to own their roles and responsibilities and to deliver. They not only have a CAN-attitude but a WILL-attitude, which is critical at any job. They are resourceful, creative, and, moreover, they are committed.

Let's take into consideration when evaluating candidates and selecting project team members. Research tells us that a good gender balance is associated with performance improvements among senior management teams; thus, gender is an aspect to consider when selecting candidates. In teams where either men or women are a minority, the minority group is unlikely to flourish. They are less satisfied and less committed to their work and teams. With this, it might be a good idea for you to get a good balance of both men and women in your project team.

While there is a popular comical suggestion that men and women are from different planets; however, in the universe of project management, men and women live on the same planet, Earth. On planet Earth, men and women tend to have certain significant differences in strengths and weaknesses. Understanding these differences will help you in the selection process. Let's look at some general suggestions as to how the genders differ in the work setting. These are stereotypes and broad generalizations, you will need to analyze people individually, this section will just give you some new things to think about when doing your analysis.

Working in Teams

Men and women differ in teamwork by the way they embrace their role in the group. For most men, being a good team player is knowing their position and doing their part well. For most women, being a good team player means having a harmonious and collaborative work relationship. If you want independent and conscientious team players, research suggests you can count on men to deliver at all cost. But if you want team players who place a strong value on unity and teamwork, you might want to bet on the female players.

Problem-Solving

In general, women tend to seek advice and opinion from others before coming to a decision on their own and tend to be more engaged with others when coming up with solutions. On the other hand, men have a tendency to try to figure things out on their own and analyze situations internally.

Group Dynamics

Men and women tend to approach group structure differently. Men are more likely to adhere to a hierarchy whereas women tend to look at groups from an equal perspective. Men like clarity knowing who the boss is and where everyone else fits in the ladder. Women, however, prefer to work in a level field where everyone gets an equal chance to be seen and heard.

It can also help you to understand the differences between generations. Now, we have four different generations working alongside each other–the Traditionalists, the Baby Boomers, Generation X, and the Millennials. The distinct characteristics of the people from each age group are rather significant and having a comprehensive understanding of these differences can help you select the right people and avoid challenges within your team.

The Traditionalist Generation (born between 1925 and 1945)–If you want to build a team whose work ethic and value is based heavily on hard work, respect for authority, and conscientiousness, you can rely on the Traditionalists. They are well defined by their name. This is because these individuals were raised in the time where hierarchy, conformity, and rules were highly valued.

Baby Boomers (born between 1946 and 1964)–Baby boomers are highly industrious. They value their careers and believe that success is achieved through hard work. They have a desire to constantly improve the quality of their works and products.

Generation X (born between 1965 and 1981)–Here comes the generation that began to value work-life balance. Generation X'ers are creative and have the drive to be self-reliant. They have high tendencies to be independent and autonomous.

The Millennials / Generation Y (born between 1982 and 2000)–The Millennials are your multi-tasers. They believe that their careers should have a meaning and a purpose bigger than it should. Millennials are likely to be motivated and inspired, given that they are put in the work environment where they are empowered.

Personality is also a helpful factor in finding the right people for your team. You must find the right personality types that will match the project, the job roles, and the personalities of yourself and the other members of the team. A highly effective team is made up of the right combination of diverse personalities. In selecting your team members, you should understand the kind of personality types and ensure that you can cultivate a work atmosphere that will allow all personality types to perform effectively and develop professionally. Let's talk about some ideal personality types you would want to have in your team.

The Leader

This is probably the personality type you will also fall into. The Leader types are the visionaries. They have the eye for an expansive vision of the project, from the planning stage to execution to the result. Leaders are the problem-solvers. They find ways to mediate conflicts and have the will to facilitate open communication among team members. The Leader is also a strong mentor–one who knows how to delegate the tasks and empower team members to step up.

The Team Player

The team player is a more extroverted individual who has the talent of bringing a team together. They are the more energetic and enthusiastic types–

always eager to work together and work for the common good. In times of conflict, they are often the pacifists who help mend loose knots and make sure that everyone works harmoniously. When someone needs help, you can expect the team player to step up and lend a hand.

The Investigator

In a project team, it will help you to have the investigator personality type. These are the people who always have questions—but not in a demeaning way. They are the ones who initiate critical thinking—and they find their own answers as well. They will provide information that can help you and your team come up with more and better solutions to problems you might face along the way.

The Professional

As we discussed, there are a number of advantages in getting a diverse group of individuals with various talents and skills. It's important, however, that you have at least one Professional personality type on board. This is the person you can rely on for knowledge and expertise in the field. In times where your project hits a technical bump, you can count on the Professional to be your subject matter expert.

The Communicator

The connectors previously discussed fall under the Communicator personality type. The Communicators are your go-to people when your project needs to convey information, send out updates, and a request for assistance from other departments and parties outside your team. They are natural at reaching out to other people and establishing connections with others. They have a certain charm that can persuade just about anyone to extend a hand when the team needs it. Also, they have a wide network and usually knows someone your team can reach out to in times of need.

The Analyst

The Analyst type is your go-to person in deal breaker situations. They are often the more objective kind of people and can be trusted to make rational call and decisions. They are able to look at situations in an objective light, which makes them good problem solvers and decision-makers. They may be mistaken as pessimists or cynics, but Analysts who are motivated (with the right WANT, WAY, and WILL); you can trust that they have the project's best interest at heart.

The Creative

The Creative personality types may not always be the most organized or the clearest communicators, but you can rely on them to bring fresh and innovative ideas to the table. They are imaginative and unconventional. Your team can really benefit from the Creatives because they are often inspired and insightful and can lead the team to produce outstanding work.

Briefly, when selecting the right team players, you need to prepare the following:

A detailed resource plan: This outlines the skills needed, and the expected duration or time frame. Metaphorically, this lays out the big picture of the house you are aiming to build as a team and where each person fits in the construction process. This plan should include everyone involved in the project and not just the project team members, but partner experts, collaborating departments, and the executives and management teams as well.

A comprehensive role description: This should include clearly defined responsibilities, tasks, and goals to be discussed and agreed upon before hiring. It may feel overwhelming to draft the job descriptions, but it will really help you select the right people who are a true fit to your project goals, to the team culture you desire, and to the position itself. This will also help you avoid potential gaps in the execution of your project in case you miss a skill set needed for a task. Note down the technical and professional competencies you need for your project. Additionally, include also the soft skills needed.

Semi-structured interview questions: It will help to prepare hypothetical questions that can assess a candidate's analytical thinking skills. Situational questions about different types of possible scenarios and various roles will give you an idea about their character and how they behave in these types of circumstances.

The selection criteria should also include personality and behavior. These personal aspects complete the puzzle of the more comprehensive profile of a candidate. Personal attributes give us a glimpse of how an individual behaves in different situations such as working with a team, handling stress, accepting criticisms, celebrating successes and dealing with people.

To save your project and yourself from trouble, you can do your own research on potential candidates by doing the following:

Take a look at their online presence on social media.
Talk to their former and present colleagues and co-workers.
Consult with their managers and leaders.
Seek out their character references and ask about work behaviors and attitudes.
Check on their previous work accomplishments and achievements that are not on their resumes.

Don't be afraid to go out of your way and use non-conventional techniques of screening potential team members to have a better understanding of who they are and how well they will fit in the project and the team.

Actively listen to your candidate's words. Analyze their initial interaction pitch. Pay attention to how they approach you and assess the content of his answers to your questions. See how the discussion evolves and take note of recurring themes in their statements. From there, you can deduce their attitudes and motivations. Also, check for non-verbal cues.

As a project manager, you are the driver of the bus. When your passengers seem to be amiss to the destination or the journey itself, you might need to do some introspection and evaluate your own role and performance in the team. Try asking yourself the following:

Are you setting a good example to demonstrate the type of team players the project needs?
Are you genuine, kind, and patient?
Do you seek to understand others?
Do you have the way, the will, and will want to get to the destination?

It's not only important to get the best people on board. It also matters if the people actually want to be there, if they know their destination, if they know whom they are riding with and if they understand the journey, and lastly if they enjoy the ride.

CHAPTER 3 MANAGING UP

"It doesn't make sense to hire smart people and tell them what to do. We hire smart people so they can tell us what to do." – Steve Jobs

During job interviews, managers would often ask us, "Tell me about yourself. What's your leadership style?" They do this to understand what kind of workers we are and to gauge if we were the type of people they can work effectively with. But how often does our manager tell us about himself or herself and what their leadership style is?

Managing up is a concept that simply means managing your manager. This doesn't mean acting as his boss; rather, this means understanding how your manager manages, learning how he works, and finding and agreeing on ways on how you can work in accordance with his leadership styles for your project to succeed with excellence. Managing up is a symbiotic approach in managing your relationship with your manager, no matter what your opinion of him or her is.

Realistically, not all managers will make this so easy for you. To be honest, there are individuals in managerial positions who are not competent, qualified, or capable in their seat at the organization. We often hear horror stories about people leaving their jobs because of bad bosses. Sometimes, great talents quit their jobs not because they don't like what they do, but because they can't seem to work well with their managers. This is extremely frustrating and can limit career opportunities and professional growth. This shows how much managers can affect employees not just in terms of performance but in morale and job satisfaction as well. In fact, some studies have shown that if given a choice, a significant number of employees would rather get a new boss than get a raise. However, even if your boss has flaws and shortcomings, making your relationship work and managing up will be beneficial to you, to your team, and to your project.

The relationship between a boss and his subordinate is often fragile. Of course, we want to keep our jobs. But it's not always easy with the pressures of meeting targets and expectations, plus the feeling of having your boss' eyes always on you, as if waiting for you to mess up. We know our bosses hold the strings on which our jobs hang, so we want to be careful as if we're walking on landmines when working with them. We always want to put our best foot forward and constantly prove our place in the organization. On the other end of it, however, your boss is actually concerned about your performance, constantly checking if you are working to the best of your potential. They are also concerned with themselves and with workplace morale as they are responsible for turnover and productivity.

In project management, your relationship with your boss can seriously make or break you. Your project is more dependent on your boss than it is on you because your boss holds the key to all the factors that will come into play for the success of your project. If you're unable to manage your relationship with your boss well, you might place your project in serious jeopardy. However, establishing a harmonious connection with your boss where you both can work in your individual ways and have a sense of understanding and respect for your differences will give you the superpower to succeed in your project.

A lack of support from upper management is often identified as the number one reason why projects fail. Consequently, upper management support is one of the biggest determinants of the success of any project. The kind of support needed from top management varies across industries, but the existence of management support practices can be determined through the following:

1. The upper management had a hand in starting your project. This means the upper management saw the need for the project and initiated it.

2. Your boss, or a member of the upper management team is involved in the planning phase and makes time to be present in project-related meetings and gatherings, such as the project kick-off conference and other major events.

3. Your boss and the upper management team has a comprehensive understanding of the project goals, objectives, and direction.

4. Your boss or a member of the upper management team participates in succession planning exercises for the project.

In technical terms, you need your manager's support for the following items:

1. To clearly define strategic objectives. Your manager is in the position and has the power to help you set clearly defined strategies to achieve your project goals.

2. Project funding. This is among the most critical aspects of your project. You will need as much support you can to ensure that your project is sufficiently funded, and it's your boss who can control the funding mechanisms, managing the budget, costs, and overall financial impact.

3. Project resources. Your manager is your partner in making this happen; she has the power to influence functional teams, get you a good pool of candidates, and help you get the right people on board.

4. Decision-making. In making critical decisions, you want your boss to be on your side, right? Upper management teams may not always see things from your perspective; they might have different opinions and lean towards choices that differ from preferences. When you have a good relationship with your manager, you can have your opinions voiced through him and have an indirect influence on the decision-making process within the upper management.

5. Damage control. In unfortunate circumstances where your project runs into trouble, an unsupportive manager is less likely to assist in resolving your issue. When things go wrong, you'd want your boss to be there to back you up.

6. Cross-departmental support. More often than not, your project will need the cooperation of other departments. In many cases, project managers encounter a number of challenges in getting people from other departments to help out, especially if their direct managers are not actively involved in

your project. You can try, of course, and your connector team players might be able to work their magic. However, one way to ensure their support is for your boss to influence upper management teams and get them on board.

With these points in mind, we can see why it's important to manage up. The better you understand your manager, the stronger your relationship is, and more importantly, the happier your boss is.

Take a look at how Harry Hogarth learned this critical skill in this short story.

Harry Hogarth awoke to the sound of the alarm on a rainy morning in his double-bed beside his wife Lauren. He was in his usual waking posture – hunched up in the fetal position, tuck-kneed in an embryonic self-embrace. Lauren had unconsciously (he hoped) pulled the entirety of the duvet onto her side of the bed and was encased in a small mountain of bed-ware. She had a serene smile on her face as warming as the sheets that covered her, a smile that instantaneously vanished when she opened her eyes and looked at her husband's huddled figure beside her, and its shivering outwards-pointing rump.

Harry slammed the alarm off and started getting himself ready for his job at the GoodFlush Sewage Company. He left for the bathroom, but not before Lauren reminded him to pack a healthy lunch for their son Michael.

He showered under a nozzle that ejected water that, at best, could be described as bordering on tepid since he still hadn't called a technician to fix the hot water heater. He was dreading yet another day at GoodFlush and the multitude of terrible jobs, his boss Lenny Spittle would throw his way, and that dread kept him from exiting the shower when he knew he should. Eventually, he got out and predictably, he was running late. He had to rush the lunch for Michael, jamming with his thumb a slice of baloney into the hole of an uncut bagel, and for something healthy, he snapped a raw carrot into halves. Lauren watched with disdain as Harry rushed out the house so fast she did not get to ask him if he'd fixed the guttering above the front door. She got her answer when she saw Harry drenched head-to-toe as he slammed the door shut.

At work Lenny Spittle, without so much as a cursory 'hello', threw an intimidatingly thick folder on his desk for the project on the re-fit of new smell-proof manhole covers at their main sewage control plant. Last month the plant was sanctioned on grounds for environmental damage after an adventurous cow in a nearby field toppled over and died after wandering perilously close to the plant. Spittle walked off and Harry watched with seething jealously as Spittle started a good-natured conversation with Ollie, the well-respected employee currently in charge of the lucrative deal GoodFlush would be making with the Vacation Inn Hotel Company in the upcoming weeks.

Harry lamented his position in the office and wondered why he was never put in charge of the good projects, a question not wondered by anyone else since they knew Harry was prone to routinely going over his budgets and past his schedules. The manhole cover re-fit should have been finished last week, and it was generally agreed among the office that Ollie could have had the job done and dusted before lunchtime.

Harry's team member in charge of purchasing the new covers had the opportunity to get a good deal right at the start of the project but turned it down on the grounds of its premium-level costs. Harry had warned him against accepting anything other than a cheap bargain. This bargain never materialized, but Harry didn't communicate this to his team member in charge of the labor at the plant site, who prematurely booked the workers to fit the non-existent covers. Subsequently, there was a sorry scattering of spanner-wielding laborers standing around at the plant, lobbing apples at the cows whilst being paid for the privilege. Spittle nearly had a fit when he found out, demanding to know why Harry hadn't just managed his expectations on finding a seller, pointing out: "Do you know how much that sanction cost is?! A few premium manhole covers are peanuts in comparison. Don't make me have to do your job for you, Harry. If I wanted to do your job, I'd fire myself, then re-hire myself on a much lower wage, which I'm not going to do for obvious reasons. Capiche?"

Harry's requirement to lead his team to be more productive this week got off to a bad start. For a lengthy period in the morning, his team found him curiously absent. Needing his guidance, they searched the office and rang the reception desks on multiple floors to no avail. When he did re-appear his reason given for his absence was an important boardroom meeting. This was, of course, a lie since he'd just spent the last forty minutes in the bathroom counting the number of sheets in a roll of toilet paper to stave off his sense of dread at returning to the office.

Once his team had been given their tasks, they went about their jobs somewhat carelessly, resulting from a lack of given direction, and little faith in their weak-willed manager. One of them, Izzy, then came up to him at 2PM asking if she could leave early, stating her grandma needed a ride to the Bingo hall. Izzy still hadn't generated any interest in the selling of the old manhole covers yet, but Harry figured they were already so far behind that another few hours couldn't matter much, and let her go.

Unsurprisingly for Harry, this new week didn't start out any more productive than his others did, and he went home dejected and stressed, walking by his overflowing bins and under his spouting gutter as he went. Once inside he began his customary whining about his job to Lauren, who had to go to bed early on account of a sharp headache—a headache that curiously disappeared the moment she got into the bedroom. Without Lauren to listen, he then began airing his woes to Michael, but once Michael started crying Harry relented and just put on Spongebob Squarepants. He silently wished he too could just be a sponge. No-one shouts at a sponge.

The next day when Harry got to work, he noticed a man in the office he hadn't seen before; a man with a long, grey ponytail and a peaceful demeanor. Upon seeing Harry, he walked up and introduced himself as Cid Allen, and said he was there to mentor Harry for the next few days. Harry wasn't happy at first and resented being thought of as needing a mentor. However, he warmed to Cid after finding out he'd been a lead guitar in the 70's rock band 'Giant Helicopter,' and complimented him on some of their choice tracks Harry still had to this day on his MP3 player.

The most obvious difference between the two men to any observer was, besides the two-foot ponytail, their outward demeanor. Harry sat hunched at his desk, a bundle of nerves, visibly perspiring as he blundered his directives to his apathetic team. Cid, on the other hand, was calm, collected and confident. Ten years of playing to live audiences made him fearless, and ten years of thankful audiences sharing their special cigarettes made him immune to stress.

With a warm smile, Cid began explaining to Harry the benefits of 'Managing Up,' which he explained as: "Making your boss' job easier by essentially managing your manager." The first point of this was to "anticipate what they would ask of you, and act accordingly without needing to be asked." Harry thought about this for a moment and, after overhearing the boss complain about his piles, went to the store on his lunch break and bought a comfy rubber ring that he then placed on the boss's chair. Cid said this wasn't exactly what he meant, but did concede it was a nice touch. Cid pointed out that what the boss needed right now was for the project to be finished already, and instead of bothering him with how to get it done, he should be driving his team to start getting results ASAP.

At that moment Izzy walked up again at 2PM with a story about how her boyfriend's car had broken. Cid coolly told her to finish selling the covers and said he hoped her boyfriend had money for the bus. Izzy wasn't happy about it but Harry noticed something about her subsequent disposition around Cid—an air of respect, something he'd never personally felt from any of his team.

Cid then discovered after a few frank questions with Harry and his team that this was a frequent move from Izzy, and Cid then went about showing Harry how the rest of his team were overworked, filling in the slack from Izzy, and the results showed this. And following a particularly enthralling conversation with Sammy, the guy in charge of the legislation of the project, Cid swapped his role with Izzy's. Sammy was a natural, and his instinctive sociability and witty charm got their covers sold at a good price within the hour.

Cid's next point of Managing Up was understanding the correct way to discuss problems with your boss, and Harry had something at that moment that he wanted help with. The new covers had been purchased by now, but the company they purchased from had sent out the wrong size and were refusing to accept responsibility. Harry knew his boss well enough to know that he didn't have time to be asked for help on his employee's projects. But what Spittle did like was hearing a question that led to self-learning for the inquisitive party.

So, when Harry knocked on his boss's door he asked: "Which of our books on company legislation deals with purchased goods?" Spittle waited a minute to see if some kind of punch line was coming but when he (eventually) realized Harry was serious and was actually trying to do half a decent job, calmly told him which book to look in. Harry left, and the boss relaxed, comfortable knowing that Harry was growing as an employee and comfortable in his soothing rubber ring. Harry then gave that book to Izzy (in her new role of legislation) and, as an avid reader of books, she quickly consumed the knowledge and was on the phone with their seller shortly afterward. The company admitted their responsibility in the eyes of the law, replaced the covers the same day, and offered an apologetic discounted price on GoodFlush's next purchase.

In almost no time the project was progressing at leaps and bounds, and Harry actually found himself with Sammy having no more work to do. This then led in nicely to Cid's final point of Managing Up – Becoming a well-rounded source of help. Harry, knowing he had some spare manpower, involved Sammy in the ongoing negotiations with the Vacation Inn. Sammy's charisma and offer of the utilization of the discount for a whole re-fit of the hotel's manhole cover impressed their management, and they fast-forwarded the whole deal by two weeks.

By the end of the day, Harry felt like a new man, rejuvenated at the sight of his project rapidly approaching completion. He thanked Cid for his help and Cid bowed his head, asking for nothing more in return than for Harry to come to see his new band playing covers of Nickleback songs at the bar downtown. Harry said he'd think about it.

A month later Harry was known as a revelation in the building, completing projects with mechanical efficiency, and he even overtook Ollie as the go-to man for project management. Oddly enough Ollie then becomes prone to some unusually long bouts in the bathroom.

Harry would go home satisfied at the end of the day, remaining dry as he walked in the door since he had the guttering fixed. He had a steaming hot shower now the electrician had been in and then sat down in front of the TV with Lauren and Michael sat beside him on the sofa. Finally, he had things in order, and when he turned to smile at Lauren she smiled back, happy in her finely-structured home. She even stopped stealing the duvet in the night... Well, most of the time.

Understand your boss

As a project manager, you know how crucial it is to have a strong understanding of your project. But in managing up, you must understand your boss as well. This means getting to know their working context, personal mission, values, goals, objectives, pressures and challenges, their strengths and weakness, their work- and communication styles, their metrics and measures of success.

The same way that your project team members have different personalities that you must understand to work well with them, you must not forget that your manager also has her personal and unique characteristics. Here are some questions you might want to consider to better understand your boss:

How does she communicate with her subordinates?
What is her preferred work style?
Is she on build-up mode or cost-cutting crunch-time?
Does she face conflict head-on or does she allow it to resolve itself in time?
Is she the confrontational type or does she have an avoiding personality type?
Does she like to conduct regular meetings and expect time-to-time updates or does she prefer a onetime report on your progress?
Does she micromanage or is she hands-off with you and your team?
Does your boss want to see data first before discussing or does she want to talk before seeing the data for herself?

Effective leaders are strong in empathy–putting one's self in the shoes of others. In managing up, try to look at the situation from the eyes of your manager whenever possible. To better understand your manager, you must know what she cares about. This will help you put into perspective your observations about her behavior, attitude, and decisions.

All the little and big details you understand about your boss will give you a better idea on how to work with her. When your boss is being difficult, chances are she's dealing with a lot of stress and she's unsure of how to deal with it. This is normal, and if you can empathize, you will know not to take this personally. Work is a stressful place, and your boss is not an exception from feeling the pressures from the job.

This also points to the importance of being aware of your own leadership and work-styles. If you differ in preferences and you feel your differences will be a challenge in meeting your goals, this first step is a way to identify areas of concern that you can discuss with your boss to arrive at a win-win solution.

Communicate with your boss

To begin your upward influence, you must learn to communicate with your boss. To start with, find out from your boss what success means to her and what her measures of success are. You need to make sure that you have a clear understanding of this to check that you are meeting your boss's expectations. Not all managers will systematically provide you with the information that you need. In this case, you'll have to pull it out of them.

If you haven't ever done so, prepare a list of items you want to discuss with your manager and set an official meeting to have a sit-down with her. This conference will be just the first of many, but it will be critical because this is your opportunity to go over expectations and have a constructive dialogue about the best ways to work together and manage your team.

You can start by validating what you already understand about her based on your initial assessment. Ask her directly what her management style is. Pay close attention and listen to what works well for you and what you might need to work out with her as a compromise. For example, your boss might require daily meetings for accomplishment reports. However, as a project manager, you may prefer to work independently to meet your own deadlines. You can consult with her if the meetings can be decreased to twice a week rather than daily. In doing this, you must keep in mind that your boss is on your side and she wants you to succeed in the project. There is a strong chance that she will adjust to provide what you need for you to do so. At this point, you can also grab the chance to explain to her how you work best and what kind of management style will help you perform at your maximum. This might seem a bit overwhelming. You might worry that giving your boss suggestions on how to manage you will give her a bad impression of you trying to overpower her, which is why you must be careful with your approach in doing this. It takes a lot of self-awareness to know what to say, and you must be careful and courageous to get your message across. It may seem difficultly at first, but talking about how to work with you will help both of you in the long run.

In situations where you feel that your boss misheard or didn't hear you at all, muster up the courage to speak to her and explain. While being a project manager entails 100% objectivity, in cases where you need to reconnect with your boss and straighten out any issue, it may not hurt to speak from the heart. In a calm and professional manner, don't be hesitant to use "I" lines, such as, "I was upset by what happened. I feel _____. I want to understand your side better. Did you mean by _____?" By showing your boss your desire to maintain strong and open communication with her, you are presenting yourself as a leader who has a strong work ethic and is able to openly discuss issues and clear up any miscommunication.

In communicating with your boss, keep in mind that communication styles vary among individuals. It's important to know how to open a conversation and negotiate with your boss to effectively meet both of your needs. Try to identify if your boss is a "reader" or a "listener." Readers understand better when they get to see the data for themselves before you talk to them. Listeners understand better when information is discussed to them first before being presented with the data. A boss who is a listener will probably set aside your document and will ask you directly, "Are we in trouble or not?" A boss who is a reader, on the other hand, is unlikely to be convinced by a quick conversation. Knowing which type your boss is will save you time and energy in communicating with her and getting favorable results. Also, it will help you get far in managing up.

When we say communicate with your boss, we also mean to communicate with them honestly and immediately. Make sure you don't leave any bad surprises for your boss to find. If any problem comes up in any phase of the project, don't wait until the last minute to inform your boss.

In project management, clarity is your best friend. When dealing with your manager, try to make your message as clear and as concise as possible. Don't be afraid to be straightforward, especially in critical situations. Whether in person or via email, use the fewest words as possible in making your point. This will make it easier for your boss to understand what you mean and to give you feedback faster\

Build a relationship with your Boss

Strong, open communication is your door to a strong relationship. In the same manner that you want to have trust, respect, and understanding within your project team, you also want to have the same things between you and your manager. Build a relationship with your manager. First, think of your manager as an ally who helps you get the wheels of your project turning, not as an overseer who merely watches you and waits for you to screw up. Remind yourself that your manager wants you and your project to succeed. She has the resources you need, has the interest of the project and your team at heart, has the capacity to sort out any interdepartmental issues, and has the voice to make decisions that will help your project.

Because your relationship with your boss is that of mutual dependence, you must remind yourself that in the same way your boss wants you to succeed, your priority should always be to make your boss successful. This concept of reciprocity makes the heart of your relationship with your manager. To invest further in your relationship with your manager, do what you can to make her look good, by doing this, you are not only lifting your boss up, but you lift yourself as well.

The ideal relationship between you and your boss are one where you both are able to communicate openly and from the heart. This makes confrontations and other difficult conversations uncomplicated and more productive. Also, do acknowledge your boss for what she does for the project, for the team, and for you. A "Thank you" can go a long way. Remember that your manager is human, just like you and everyone else in your team. People are more satisfied, more engaged, and more motivated when they feel appreciated for what they do.

A strong relationship does not mean that you must be constantly in touch with your boss. A lot of people easily fall into the trap that they must be available to answer to their bosses on a 24/7 basis. Therefore, it's important to remember to set healthy boundaries. When we speak of strong relationships with your boss, we are talking about the professional kind. You must be careful in drawing a fine line and setting boundaries firmly and respectfully. In managing your boss, you must be your own boss as well.

For many people, there is a certain period in their day where they are most relaxed and have their guards down. Keep an eye out to know your boss' schedule and work patterns to find those windows of opportunities where you can initiate conversations that are both professional and personal to get to know her better. If you think your boss would be agreeable to having a meal with you, consider inviting her to establish rapport. If you feel that either of you will find the situation uncomfortable, have another co-worker or your project team members join you. The stronger your bond is with your boss and the more cohesive your team is, the higher your chance is to get its trust, respect, and support.

Be truthful with your boss

We've all heard of one of the golden rules: honesty is the best policy. In building a good relationship and keeping open communication with your boss, you must be truthful. Transparency is one of the core values of a true leader. To get your boss to trust you, she must know that you can be honest and open with her.

Frustrations, grievances, and disappointments are normal. These are sentiments which you can express to your boss–but in a positive and appropriate manner. Again, effective communication is key. Learn the ways on how you can phrase your concerns to make your boss understand them from your perspective and turn them into suggestions that will work for both of you. Let´s say you're unhappy about the lack of an organized agenda for weekly meetings. You can recommend to your boss preparing a list of discussion points for your future meetings. Don't be afraid to express your thoughts and ideas but be mindful to speak out in a constructive way that will not cause problems in your project, but rather, help you and your boss make improvements in the way you work.

One of the basic ways to show integrity is to keep promises. You want your boss to know that he can trust you to get the job done–and to get it done right. When you take on a responsibility, whether it's as small as sending an email before leaving the office or it's as big as meeting with a client, you must make sure that you follow through fervently.

You have probably heard of the popular advice to "under promise and over deliver." While it is good to impress customers and can significantly increase satisfaction and exceed customer expectations, this will not work as well in managing your manager. Of course, you want your manager to be thrilled with your performance and results. However, research has shown that over-delivering may be a waste of effort. Doing this will only condition your manager to expect that level of performance every time, hence increasing the standards of functioning to a degree higher than was originally agreed on. Doing less than agreed upon will give the impression that you are now under-performing. Experts then advise focusing on investing in giving realistic promises and keeping them rather than exceeding them.

Open communication is extremely vital in establishing a good relationship with your manager–in this section, we emphasize on the term "open." This behavior must remain, even when delivering the bad news that you know will upset your boss or dampen his day; you must be courageous in informing him immediately. Don't assume that your boss already knows any important news that involves you, your team, and your project. If you feel that this information is valuable and significant, you must take the lead in communicating this. Again, the best way to go is to make your message coherent, concise, and clear.

It's safe to expect that your project might hit a bump in the road. Project management includes a painstaking risk analysis to identify potential threats and prevent any hazard or pitfall. However, sometimes you meet the inevitable setbacks and unintentional oversights. When you or your team makes a mistake or fails to a certain extent, you must be responsible enough to take accountability and be upfront with your boss in owning up to the situation. Don't play the pointing game or blame others. Be honest and don't make excuses. Demonstrate your accountability by explaining where you went wrong, how you plan to correct it, and what actions you will take to ensure it won't happen again. You will minimize any damage to your credibility and any dent in your relationship with your boss by being truthful and owning your problems.

In line with this, don't be shy about asking for help from your boss. If the situation is out of your hands or it's one you haven't dealt with before and you are unsure about your action plans, seek out advice. Remember that your boss is also your mentor. You don't need to look far to find one of the best people you can learn from. So, go ahead and don't be afraid to admit that you need his help from time to time.

Another tricky situation in managing up is when you disagree with your boss, which can sometimes be inevitable. It's fine to have disagreements if you know how to deal with it in a respectful and professional manner. Be open with your boss, and don't be offensive with your approach. Remind yourself that you and your boss share a common goal and you both have the best interest of your project at heart.

Here's another way to make it easier in being honest with your manager: don't forget that no matter how different they are from you; they are human just like you. Wrapping your mind around this often-forgotten fact makes it less difficult to see your manager as a real person who can understand how you feel. This can break down the invisible wall between you and your manager. Remind yourself that like you, your boss has her own emotions – anxieties, hopes, frustrations, and the like. Your boss is not just a person who provides targets, evaluates performance, and decides who is promoted.

Be an example of your own ideal boss

There's an old saying that goes "actions speak louder than words." Maintaining open communication doesn't just stop at having regular discussions with your boss. You must also play the part of the kind of boss you want to have. Keep your commitments. Be present and transparent with your team. Speak with the right balance of conviction and passion.

In times of crisis, when everything is falling apart, your role as a project manager is to keep things under control. Excellent leaders not only have the ability to remain calm in chaos, but they can address the situation with a sound of reason and objectivism.

Problem solvers will always find solutions to every problem. Problem creators will always find problems in every solution. As a leader, be a problem solver. There will always be problems with every project. When presenting it to your boss, don't go to him with a list of problems and your complaints. Do your best to deliver the situation with no drama and with at least one strategy or practical suggestion to deal with it.

Take the initiative to fulfill your responsibilities as the project team's leader and as your boss' follower even without being asked. Send regular updates, keep your boss posted on your project milestones, send meeting invitations, furnish performance reviews of your team, and provide regular feedback and acknowledgments.

If you are the type who constantly focuses on the bad, such as the gaps, the flaws, the errors, this can bring everyone down. It leads to a contagious feeling of frustration, anger, hopelessness, and irritability. This will affect your mood, your team's mood, and your boss's mood, affecting overall performance and productivity in the team. Be a consistent source of positivity. Think, speak, and act positively at all times. A can-do attitude will motivate others and make them feel good. Seeking to find the silver lining in every dark cloud will drive everyone to be positive–this includes your boss.

In project management courses, you may have encountered discussions about manager-employee relationships. Understanding reporting relationships are crucial in project management. Upon receiving any role in a project, you must be clear whom you will report to. There are different ways that organizational hierarchy is structured. Let's take a quick look at each one:

Flat / Horizontal Structure: A horizontal structure is often seen in smaller and start-up companies. A flat organizational structure is less of a hierarchy and is called flat because it gives employees access to resources and decision-making. It empowers employees to collaborate and to make choices and move on their prerogative. This speeds up operations and enables the organization to innovate faster. However, horizontal organizations may be challenged when teams begin to grow and employees increase in number.

Hierarchical / Vertical Structure: The vertical structure is more traditional and more ordered in nature. It follows a chain of command where teams report directly to a manager. The hierarchical organization often, if not always, observes formal communication, decision-making, and other organizational transactions and processes. Because of these policies in engagement, the vertical structure can be slow to change and can pose certain limitations. Managers are also at risk of being overload in handling different teams and individuals at the same time.

Matrix Structure: Matrix structures are also referred to as the dotted-line structure. It is a more complicated organizational system where team members often report to more than one person. Oftentimes, in matrix structures, several individuals have multiple roles and functions which require them to report to different managers. This is not uncommon in project management. For example, you have an IT person on your team, in addition to reporting to you, his project manager, he might also be required to report the IT manager whose department is also involved in your project to a certain extent. In the organizational chart, this may be represented by a dotted line relationship linking your team member to the IT manager.

A matrix structure can be tricky, especially when people who have multiple bosses. Let's look at your hypothetical IT team member. As his project manager you are responsible for giving his assignments, but he receives other instruction from the IT manager. If you both have different styles and expectations in terms of output, he will find himself in hot water. Should you find yourself in this kind of situation, remember that these are your team players, and as their project manager, it is your responsibility to help them get their job done for the success of the project. To avoid getting in a box like this, here's where you can apply what we've discussed so far in this chapter; manage up. As a project manager, establish a good working relationship with the IT Manager. First, understand him; What are his goals? What is his leadership style? What kind of negotiating style works on him? Next, communicate. Set an appointment where you can personally discuss expectations and common goals. Afterward, agree on how you can work together. You can also set certain boundaries in terms of reporting relationships for him. Lastly, maintain a good rapport with him, and to all other heads of different departments that are involved in your projects, such as Finance, Admin, or Human Resources.

In cases where you are under a matrix organization structure, you must know whose reporting line is most powerful and has the most influence among the different managers. It's also critical that you are informed of the responsibilities your managers have, such as who sets the main project objectives, who conducts performance appraisals, who is responsible for internal and external communications, etc.

Virtual Structures: As the global workforce continues to innovate with the growth of technology, more and more organizations are adopting flexible work arrangements such as working virtually. Virtual organizations are gaining popularity as it has several advantages with respect to business costs, productivity, and individual and collective well-being and satisfaction. This may often limit your communication as a project manager, especially if you are under a virtual matrix structure. In virtual structures, if your boss hasn't set a regular schedule for updates and calibration, you might want to bring it up as a suggestion and set a recurring meeting at a time most convenient for both of you. This shows initiative and respect for her as your leader. It will also keep your manager in the loop as you keep her up to date with the progress of the project even if she is not physically present. Moreover, should a problem arise in any phase of the project, it's vital that you report it immediately to your manager. This builds a sense of trust and will strengthen your relationship with your boss, helping you manage up.

In the organization structure types, we discussed, you might deduce that none of the four are without risk to certain loopholes in reporting relationships. There are unclear and confounding connections in some management structures which you will want to avoid. Here are some:

The Loop: Gina reports to Mark. Mark reports to Catherine. Catherine reports to Gina.

The Reverse: Marie is the executive manager. Lance is his associate manager. Marie often reports to Lance about operations-related tasks.

The Remote: Marlo reports to Beverly. Beverly reports to no one.

The Every-Which-Way: Rowel reports to Daisy. Sometimes Rowel reports to Miles. Daisy reports to David. Sometimes David reports to Rowel.

These scenarios are examples of un-clear reporting relationships. These situations can cause a serious dent in your project. An undefined organizational structure and unclear reporting lines will confuse you, your project team members, and possibly other departments who are involved in your project as well. This can lead to serious obstacles that can slow down the progress of your project if not overthrow it completely. For any concern about the structure of your project team, your manager is your ally. Manage up and use the skills we discussed in getting a clear reporting line between you and within your team. Because your manager has more power and influence, she will be the right one to ensure that you and your team have clearly defined reporting relationships that will allow you to work without complication and to focus on one project, one task, one assignment at a time.

Like most difficult situations, when in a rough patch with your boss, it's easy to get carried away and resort to negativity. Some people tend to keep their thoughts to themselves, grit their teeth, give their managers a nod and tough it out. There are some who go against their bosses and take things to their own control, leaving their manager out to get the job done. Sometimes you got to do what you got to do, they say. But often, these approaches often turn out unfavorably. Chances are this will backfire on you and there aren´t many ways to win over your manager; she is still your boss and more powerful and more influential than you. Moreover, this will cause a huge dent on your integrity as a leader and as a professional.

One of the biggest factors that lead to happiness is having strong and positive social relationships. It's no surprise that happiness can ultimately affect how we behave, how we perform, and how we interact with the people around us. In the workplace, to be the best we can be depends on how we manage our relationships–especially with our bosses. Managing up does not mean "sucking up" to your manager. Managing up may not always be easy or pleasant. There will be situations that are difficult, challenging, uncomfortable, and frustrating. Therefore, it's important to have a strong grasp of your project goals. The key is to be a highly effective leader that adds value to the project, to your team, to your bosses, and to the organization.

Don't forget, your project is also your boss' project; your team is also her team. She wants you to succeed in your project just as much as you want it for yourself. By managing not only downward toward your project team but upward too toward your manager, you can make the most out of your influence and set your project and your team up for success.

CHAPTER 4 RESPONDING TO CHANGE

"Change is the law of life. And those who look only to the past or present are certain to miss the future." -John F. Kennedy

Projects always start with a Plan. The traditional idea in project management is that the plan is the blueprint of your project. It tells you what needs to be done, how it should be done, and what you expect to have at the end of the process. When your project hits a bump along the road, you often resort back to your plan to find the best solution. However, the truth of the matter is, the project plan, no matter how calculated, intensive, and well-made will always be prone to risk and uncertainty. This is not because the plan is poorly made; there are simply inevitable factors that will require you to make changes in your plan. As cliché as it may sound, it rings true, even in projects: the only constant thing is change. With this idea in mind, it will be helpful for you to expect that your project plan and schedules will not be the same after three or six months after starting your project.

As a project leader, you should anticipate any surprises that may come your way at any point in the project phase. While we have mentioned that as a leader, your role is to be a driving force of positivity, it's equally important that you find the right balance of optimism and pragmatism. Being pragmatic entails being realistic and preparing for potential risks and changes in your project plan.

Failing to estimate potential threats can result in delays in your timeline, blurring of your project scope, adjustments in budget and costing, and numerous change requests. Needless to say, change can be difficult. When situations require a change in routine, behavior, and attitudes, you can expect that people will have a hard time. Naturally, humans are wired in a way that require a need for certainty, especially when it involves their jobs which is their livelihood. Your team members are no exception unless you, as their leader jump into this project prepared to handle these kinds of situations. Hence, as a project manager, one of the most important competencies you should be equipped with is the skill to be agile and adaptable to any change that comes your way.

Before proceeding with how to manage change, let's discuss some of the types of changes in a project or within a team or in an organization. The type of change will affect what adjustments are needed in the project.

Developmental Change: Simple modifications. This type of change focuses mostly on improving existing processes, methods, standards, and other performance conditions.

Transitional Change: Replacing something old with something new. For example, changing an existing software that analyses data gathered from your project with an upgraded program that can process more input and produce more inferences. Transitional change can apply to your project's operational systems such as processes or services.

Transformational Change: Radical change. This requires a more thorough process of change within your project. In Project Management, these situations that often require that you apply Change Management Models and use trial-and-error to identify areas of concerns and come up with strategies to change existing workplace culture. Oftentimes, transformational changes require an overhaul of the entire project plan.

As in any phase in your project, you want to be able to handle changes in an organized manner that is easy to track and monitor. A defined change process scheme will help you and your team navigate through the developments of your project that are not in the original plan to remain on the right track toward your project's ultimate goals. Here is a staged approach to processing change within a project.

Stage 1: The Proposal

The proposal stage is where the need for change is first presented. This may come from anyone involved in the project—such as yourself, the senior leadership team, your team members, or even your clients and customers. The proposal should cover the details of the change request – clearly defining the justification of the reason for the change, its description and scope, and its expected outcomes. It will help you keep proper track and documentation of the changes in your project if your company doesn't have a documentation procedure in place already. This is submitted to you as the project manager, so you can validate and move forward to the next stage.

Stage 2: Analyze and Summarize

The phase is the process of assessing the possible overall effect and results of the change on the project and drafting a summary of the impact of the proposed change. This covers budget, cost-savings, legal or regulatory implications, impact on the time frame and work schedules, availability of resources, quality of service and output, the effect on your team members' responsibilities, potential risks and issues, and effects on other project activities. If necessary, communicate with the requestor to clarify information and corroborate on ideas. With that information you can then draft your recommendation on whether to carry out the change.

Stage 3: The Decision

In decision-making, it's best for all stakeholders to be involved to a certain degree, depending on the scope of the proposed change, especially if the change will have a significant impact on the project. Get feedback from your team members, consult with your senior leaders, and confer with the clients. When people feel they are involved in the planning and decision-making, they are more likely to have a sense of accountability, embrace the change and proactively encourage others to support the decision as well. Alienating your team in this process can cost you their trust and impact the integrity of the change and other future developments.

Stage 4: Implementation

Should you arrive at the decision to accept the change, plan, schedule, and implement at a time agreed with all stakeholders. Again, it is critical that you involve your team in the planning and preparation on how to execute the changes, this will ultimately be indispensable to carrying them out

successfully.
We will discuss in detail later in this chapter.

Stage 5: Closing

At the end of the change process, ensure proper documentation and continue to monitor the adaptation of your team and other stakeholders to the change in the project. Some may adapt to change quickly while others may take more time and will need more support. In some situations, further training may be needed even after the implementation of change. A regular evaluation may also be necessary to measure success and avoid potential risks.

Lack of strong and focused leadership

Change, especially major change, will need to begin from the top. This includes not only you as the project manager but also your leaders from the senior executive teams. Employees and team members will be more likely to resist and have a negative attitude toward any change if they see and feel that their management teams do not fully support it or are not consistent with their stance on the change process. Leaders must be constant with their support for the change from the beginning until the closing for their people to walk with them throughout the entire change cycle. As the project leader, this will reflect mostly on you—on how you will communicate and implement the change.

Wrong choice of strategy or approach

The change process serves as a guide on how to manage change, but the details of your strategy for communication and implementation should be aligned with the needs of the project and the culture of your team. As a leader, you should have the necessary information to make knowledgeable assessments to determine the correct approach.

Lack of planning

If you fail to plan, you plan to fail. Implementing change, like your project itself, needs to be thoroughly planned. Planning is important to identify risk factors and potential threats that can be detrimental to your progress in the project. It will also show you how the fundamentals of your project may be affected by the change, from this, you can prepare action plans to minimize any damages to your project.

Ineffective engagement

For change to be effective, all stakeholders involved should be well-informed and on board with the expected modifications in your project. Make sure all your stakeholders are included in the change process and maintain open communication with them.

Take the lead on change

Leaders must be the first people to understand and support change. Make sure you are well-informed about the proposed changes in your project. Stay on top of every detail at every stage in the change process and ensure that all persons involved are aligned with the changes that need to be implemented. One of the most effective strategies to manage change is to condition yourself and your team to find the right balance in being both proactive and reactive.

Proactive people know the importance of being prepared. They don't wait for things to happen, but, rather, act to make things happen. They take responsibility and hold themselves accountable for any situation. They believe in their power to choose instead of being controlled by situations. They take matters into their hands. Proactive people concern themselves with the things that are within their sphere of influence, meaning the things that they can control. Be a proactive project manger.

Being proactive means acting before the situation turns into the source of a dilemma. In change management, you must be able to foresee any potential risks that can affect your outcomes and prepare to make changes in your processes to avoid this or at least ensure that they have the least negative impact as possible. Proactive leaders foresee the possible positive and negative consequences of change and incorporate these into risk reduction and management schemes. Should any issue arise, proactive people are prepared.

Reactive people, on the other hand, tend to be motivated by their external environment. This means they can act when prodded by situations as they happen. They can come up with immediate and impromptu solutions. They are likely to be resourceful and agile.

However, reactivity can spark creativity and quick-thinking. All the preparation in the world may not be enough to save you from the inevitable surprise changes in the project. There is still a slight chance that you and your team may overlook a potential risk that will surface at a point in any of the stages in the project and will require some modifications. In this case, you will need to be quick on your feet and functionally reactive.

You can expect the need for change to arise at any point in your project and being the proactive leader, you are, you can prepare for all the possible scenarios you can think of. However, you should also be able to be a reactive leader that's capable of making fast, well-informed decisions should any unforeseen risks arise in your project.

Most of the time, change is uncomfortable. Not everyone will be quick to accept change, especially when it means changing their personal routines and existing habits. Some people might use avoidance as a strategy to deal with it. In the workplace, managers may avoid opening discussions with their teams, or employees may avoid discussing it with their colleagues. This can be just as true for projects, especially in difficult situations where you'll have to present a change to your project that may interrupt the existing workflow of your team. However, while it may be difficult and uncomfortable, you must step up and deliver. As a project manager, it's your responsibility to lead the change, and one way to do this is to address the elephant in the room. You must be the one to break the ice and facilitate the discussion of change. If your team members see that their leader is uncomfortable and uncertain, chances are they will not be too enthusiastic to buy in the change.

Because change is inevitable, it's likely to happen at more than one point in your project. When it does, don't let it throw you and your team off track. Look at it positively and see it as an opportunity for you and your team to seek out solutions and constant improvements in your existing plans and processes. Challenge your team positively to think about process improvements, cost-savings, and innovative ideas. Help your team realize that change is not necessarily a bad thing. Encountering change is a chance to build resilience and to keep moving forward. Try to establish your team's mindset to focus on being problem solvers (who focus on solutions) rather than problem dwellers (who focus on setbacks). Additionally, you can turn challenges like this into a chance to bring your team together in coming up with creative strategies.

Consider your team

When the inevitable need for adjustments arise in your project, the first thing you should do is assess how your team will be affected, including the resources they require in their jobs that may be disrupted by changes. These resources may be objects, coworkers, office spaces, work schedules, or even the company's culture itself. When these objects and resources are threatened by change, it can take a toll on your team and upset productivity and morale. Make sure to note these items and prepare your proposal on how to help your team find new norms to work. Be genuinely concerned about your team and find ways to show this to them.

As soon as the request for change is received and the process begins, be mindful to pay close attention to your team and listen carefully to their inputs. As we had previously discussed, change can unsettle people, especially when it poses a threat to their work and routine. Some people may be open about their concerns, but some team members might not be comfortable sharing their anxieties; others will be strongly resistant to change. Pay close attention to their behaviors or performance. Try to understand where the resistance is coming from—whether from the change itself or another underlying issue in the project or the workplace culture. These details will help you in the next suggested approach, which is creating a communication plan. Remember the old saying; seek first to understand, then to be understood.

Create a communication plan

Communication plans are crucial to change management. If changes are not properly communicated, your team members may be misinformed with the change or misinterpret the need for it. Make sure that if there are changes in roles and tasks, these are clearly defined. Anyone assigned to driving the change must own their specific role in the change process. Your project team will probably require guidance. In your communication plan, find the correct balance to bring on change gently and encourage them into it by educating your team about the change and not dictate it to them. Help them understand and prepare them for the adjustments. You can find communication plan templates at: www.wranglingsquirrels.com/resources

To come up with the best way to change the way people work, you must first know how your people react to change. Their personality types and communication styles will help you pre-determine the best strategies to plan how to communicate to and plan the steps of change for your team. Additionally, this will also help you predict how the changes will affect your team. Perhaps you have many team members who are quick to understand and faster to adapt to modifications in your project plan whereas some might need more time to adjust and accept the change. In Chapter 2, we talked about diverse project teams. Because your team is made of different personalities, you might have to draft a communication plan where some are given more time and provided consultation opportunities to understand and accept the change.

Poor communication or the lack of it can have an adverse rather than constructive effect on your project. The kind of change also matters when drafting your communication plan. For example, in developmental changes, usually, there's no need to further explain why it's needed and why it's happening. However, transformational changes require more explanation. It will also take more time and more steps in the communication process for all individuals to get a full grasp of the expected modifications. Hence, it's equally important that you keep your team informed in the entire change process, from before, to during, to after the implementation of change. Ensure that communication lines are open, and they are aware that they are welcome to provide their input at any phase in the change process. To ensure that your team embraces the change and will not go back to the old way of doing things, check up on your people regularly and acknowledge short-term wins and successes.

One element of your communication plan that might not be explicitly included there, is the value of transparency. We go back to the first point made, take the lead in change. Be a leader and set an example of honesty for your team.

Prepare your team

Certain personality types are prone to finding comfort in a stable and routine environment. When this is disrupted, they may feel blindsided and find it difficult to adapt quickly. As the project manager, it's up to you to make sure that your team is prepared in case an immediate change is necessary for your project, whether it's a small-scale developmental change or an organization-wide transformation. Because change is unavoidable, you and your team should always be prepared. How you and your team management changes will have a major impact on the system of your project.

To fully accept the change, your team must have a clear understanding of what the change is, why there is a need for change, what its purpose and significance is, and how it will affect the outcome of the project. As a project leader, it is your task to communicate this to your team. When your team understands the reason and the rationale behind the change and how this will affect them, they are less likely to resist.

Most of the time, the best way to prepare your team is to have them trained. Conduct a Training Needs Assessment (TNA) in relation to the skills your team may need to adapt to the changes in your project, whether it's for a new system, process, or service. Make sure that your team is equipped with the necessary skills to learn and to be successful in adapting to and carrying out the change. When people feel incapacitated to do their tasks, they become frustrated. Your team members must be confident that they can do what is expected of them with the new changes in your project. Trainings are most effective when conducted before, during, and after the implementation of the change. Remember, your team needs to be well-trained for the change to be fully embraced.

Preparation often takes times. Don't expect immediate full acceptance of change. When pressured, reluctance may become stronger and the team will be less likely to embrace the change. Find out what they need. If they are in denial, present the data and educate them about the change–why it is needed and what are the expected end results from the adjustments. Allow them time to process this and provide them the support they need to prepare accordingly.

Celebrate small wins

Psychology tells us that one of the simplest ways to change behavior is through providing positive reinforcements. This suggests that celebrating small wins and rewarding efforts to accept change can make the transition smoother for you and your team. Create a plan that will allow you to publicly reward your team members who respond well to the change and actively support the new initiatives. Identify these people as your "change agents" and depict them as role models. This way, you and these "change agents" can proactively encourage others to adapt as well and get on board with your change process.

Get the right tools and prepare ahead of time

Tools are the resources needed to carry out your projects, such as physical assets, funding, timescales, and even manpower. One important tool that can come in handy when dealing with changes in your project is your contingency fund. Having a contingency fund will prepare you for anticipated changes without having to worry about ruining your financial plan. It allows you to make quick decisions on expenditures without compromising your working budget. In case you don't have a contingency fund or don't have enough of it, you may need to utilize cost management tools to assess if a request for additional funding is necessary.

Technical change management tools are readily available for your perusal online and can help you in the change process. These tools are often standardized templates that can make your change process more organized and easier to monitor. Don't disregard using checklists or process mapping to track your progress more easily, even with just minimal changes. This will help you and your team be aligned with your movements into the change process.

Changes in your project can also affect your predetermined time frames. Ideally, changes in your project plan shouldn't affect your target deadlines. If possible, you can adjust your scope to accommodate the changes, but don't adjust your timelines. However, in case this is not an option, you can use scheduling tools that can help you predict finish dates with a probability based on data. This can be useful when you present to the senior management teams and your clients the adjustments in your timelines due to the changes implemented.

Don't forget to maintain documentation of all changes in your project. Collect all change requests forms and maintain your change-logs accordingly. These are useful references that will support all the developments of your project.

Don't forget your clients

A common reason for changes in the project often comes from the end destination itself, which is your client. This frequently happens in projects where scope and requirements are not clearly defined. Sometimes, clients simply change their minds. It's perfectly normal but it can derail your progress if you are not prepared for it. As the project leader, being agile will help you manage your clients' demands and expectations and communicate with them to better deal with change. Maintaining open communication will help earn their trust.

Be mindful to draw the line between being involved and being annoying. As a project leader, you must show that you can make sound decisions in circumstances that are within your scope. You don't need to bring every little concern to them and cause them unnecessary stress. In an agile project, more focus is given to the client. As the agile team member, you should be able to change focus more frequently according to the client's needs. To cater to these ever-changing client requirements, the project team must have a proper agreement and change management process in place. Otherwise the project may exceed budgeted time and cost.

Make change simple

Flexibility is key. You want to allow yourself and your team the space to properly transition into any change. This means, not limiting adjustments to just the process but also the scope, the requirements, perhaps even the schedule, granted that you will not compromise the quality of your results.

With the authority you have as project manager, don't hesitate to make small fixes on things you have control over if this will help your team manage changes better. A good example of this a case of miscommunication and misunderstanding; if you feel that there is a gap in their understanding about the change, take the initiative to address it immediately. Provide reassuring words of guidance that can help them adjust easier. Moreover, offer solutions that you think will ease the transition phase. Also, avoid making promises in situations that are beyond your control. Giving false hopes on things outside your scope will not only be unhelpful but I can also cause a dent in your credibility as a leader.

The idea is to simplify the change process, not shorten it. Each individual deals with change at their own pace. Most of the time, you will find a pattern of the cycle of the change process: He/She learns of the change and feels discomfort at the idea of uncertainty. He/She discovers ways to adapt to change and learns how to cope. Plan your change management strategies and approaches based on your team's profile and culture to make it easier for them to accept and adapt. Especially in major adjustments, change can be complex. Make it simple and easier to implement by breaking down the process into smaller manageable steps that your team will understand quickly.

Above all else, your team will need you to validate the change by offering your support. Based on your personal assessment of their needs and the feedback they've given you, implement strategies that will support your team as they transition into the change in the project. Your presence will also be a clear message of your support. Keep your door open for your team. Some people have an instinctive fear of change. You, as their project leader, you can help them address this fear by being present and engaging in dialogues with them.

Prepare to answer questions

Your team will look to you for confidence when things become shaky. Change often does this to people. Your team is likely to have questions about the situation. They might ask how their roles and tasks will be affected. Therefore, you must be able to speak with confidence about the changes. Be transparent with your team and speak with certainty when responding to their questions. Present the data, if necessary, to assure them that you will remain on track and will meet your finish dates.

This step will be easier for you if you have already gained the trust of your team ahead of the change process. Your project team can be the most experienced in adapting changes but if they don't find you credible and trustworthy, they probably are too keen on believing that you are leading them in the right direction with the changes you are presenting. People need to trust their leaders, especially when you want them to get them on board with something new and different. Pressing change on a team who doesn't completely trust you yet may cause them to speculate ulterior motives and cut back on the little trust they might already have for you.

Remember, as the project manager, you must own every decision you make. It may seem overwhelming to think that you need to have an answer to every possible question, but your team needs to feel that you are confident with the change, so they can be convinced as well.

Get their feedback

The first person to hear your team's voice is yourself. There is a relatively good chance that your team already knows the kind of changes needed to refine your project and to improve the existing processes. Getting their input can help you craft a smooth transition plan to implement the change. Provide them with an avenue to air their thoughts, such as setting a sit-down meeting, furnishing suggestion boxes, or administering anonymous surveys. Assure them that even negative reactions are welcome; if they feel strongly about the change not being the best or right thing to do in your project at the time of the implementation, let them know that you will take their input into serious consideration.

This is crucial for you as project leader but incorporating their feedback into the change will help you get their buy-in, making it easier for them to embrace the change because they know they are a part of it. It holds everyone in the team accountable and it helps align new tasks and goals.

Inviting feedback shouldn't stop at the planning phase of the change process. Continue to ask for your team's input as the changes take place. Additionally, more than asking for their feedback, make it a point to acknowledge your team's input. There will be situations where democratic leadership may not be your best approach. Project managers will inevitably face situations where they will need to make the call and decide based on their own prerogative as leader of the project. In these cases, especially when your decision is not aligned with the opinion of most of your team, don't fail to acknowledge that their input is valuable and was taken into consideration. Make it a point to explain the need for the change and the reason why the specific decision was made. However, don't be afraid to embrace the idea that your plans for change can be changed further as well, based on the real-time feedback from your team members. Their input will serve as your data to justify supplementary adjustments to get the best possible results.

Monitor and Evaluate

Effective and successful change doesn't happen overnight. Change is a process; it takes time for teams to adapt fully and learn the ropes of new ways and processes. Most of the time, even after the change takes place, some people may still take time to get the hang of the modifications in the project. Keep an eye out for your team. Monitor their progress in the change process and evaluate their performance. Watch out for those who aren't team players and are stubbornly resistant. Provide appraisals and discuss this with each team member. Present possible ways to help them embrace the changes if they are having difficulty.

As the project manager, you must be mindful of the principles of leading change with your team. At the same time, you also play the role of the decision-maker–taking into consideration your team's morale, your objectives, and your time frames. In managing change in your project, it's your job to ensure that everyone knows what's expected of them, how they can adapt to the changes fast, and how they can make the change more successful. Set proper expectations with your team members. Even after hiring them, continue to communicate with your team about your project goals, your values, mission, and vision. Empower them in a way that they stay on their toes and do not fall into the trap of complacency and insipid comfortability in their roles. Help them embrace dynamism so when they are faced with change, they will be able to accept and adapt quickly and with ease. Additionally, train your team members to understand that change management does not end after the implementation of the change. Remember to always check on your teams, be open for any concerns, acknowledge achievements, and keep communications lines open.

The best way that you can prepare for change is to actually experience it. You must be able to go through it a couple of times to appreciate change as an opportunity to develop agility and improve your ability to adapt quickly and confidently in times of alterations or rearrangements in your project. People often resist what they do not know, and change is something uncertain which is why people fear it. In change management, there's no one-size-fits-all solution. Change and its consequences can be very unpredictable. The general goal is adapting to change with the least trouble as possible to make the adjustments and still meeting your initial objective.

Change is inevitable; growth, however, is a choice. Great project leaders know that change is ironically fixed, which is why they are always prepared for change. Great project leaders do not see changes as disruptions in the project process; great leaders keep their cool and see changes as opportunities to make adjustments for continuous improvements. Great project leaders are not afraid of changes because they believe in their team's capacity to adapt and develop with the changes.

CHAPTER 5 NEGOTIATING

"All war represents a failure of diplomacy." -Tony Benn

If there's one thing that a project manager does throughout the entire duration of the project phase, it's negotiating. Negotiation is the process of back-and-forth communication between two or more parties with the purpose to reach a mutual agreement and joint decision about differing needs or ideas. Simply put, to negotiate is to discuss and persuade others to give us something, whether in a material form or a change in behavior or in output, in exchange for something else at a reasonable cost. Not all negotiations are a you-against-me dialogue. Ideally, in a negotiation, the aim is to find a solution where all parties involved will find a mutually acceptable outcome that's for the best interest of everyone.

Project negotiations are done when you're planning the project, seeking approval for your proposals, looking to increase your budget, mobilizing your team members, or even dealing with your stakeholders. This is why successful negotiations take practice and skill because there is a lot at stake for the success of your project.

In general, negotiations can take place at any time in your project life cycle. They can be formal or informal in nature, depending on the parties involved and the purpose of the negotiation. Official project proceeding such as contracts and budgeting require formal negotiations. For minor issues such as small conflicts or use of internal resources, informal negotiations may suffice.

Negotiations fall within two basic types:

One is distributive negotiation. This is also called competitive negotiations, zero-sum, or win-lose negotiations. This is the type of negotiation where each party aims to maximize what they can get from a joint agreement. It's called competitive and win-lose because, at the end of the negotiation, there's often one party who gains more than the other, making it a battle where there is a winner who has a greater benefit, especially when the amount of the resources are fixed. Scenarios in this negotiation sometimes end where someone walks away with his or her project to be delivered in time or not (if you're negotiating about timelines), or someone walks away with an increase in his or her budget or not (if you're negotiating about cost). In distributive negotiations, the more commonly used negotiation styles are both the Hard (controlling) and the Soft (giving in) approaches. Hard bargaining is a competitive, more aggressive approach where you see the other parties as your enemies and you must win them over to get what you need from the negotiation, even if it means compromising your work relationship with the other parties. On the other hand, soft bargaining is the opposite where you become too careful not to clash with the other party in the negotiation process that you become more agreeable and more susceptible to being taken advantage of. This type of negotiation is called win-lose, but even if you win the negotiation itself, this can be bad for your project as the long-term outcome can be a lose-lose. To better understand this, let's talk about the second type of negotiation.

The second type is called the integrative negotiation process. Unlike the distributive negotiation, the integrative approach seeks to land a "win-win" scenario for all parties. The goal is to be able to achieve an agreement where each party gains a substantial amount, if not all, of what they are looking for in the negotiation. Also called the collaborative negotiation, the integrative negotiation process is ideal because it tends to produce the best results while helping you strengthen working relationships with other parties and lessen the chances of conflict. There are two steps in this approach. First, all parties will incorporate supplementary items that can be added to the overall relative value of the resources being negotiated. The objective of this step is to significantly increase the general cost and potential merits of the negotiation. Following this step is the process, which is the negotiating process of distributing the resources at hand. Because there are more items on hand, all parties have a higher chance of getting items that are valuable to them in the negotiation. If in the first step, all parties were able to expand the overall worth of the items at stake, at the end of the negotiating process, there is a good chance that all parties will walk away feeling like winners.

In project negotiation, it's better to aim for an integrative approach–to aim for a win-win outcome. As mentioned, in the long run, you will likely have more to gain by seeking out the best interests of other parties involved, such as your team members, stakeholders, and other partners.

To achieve a successful integrative negotiation, it's best to follow a third negotiation style – principled bargaining. Principled negotiators can separate personal affairs from the problem and focus on the interest of all. They know how to focus on what's at stakes, can come up with mutually beneficial options, and can decide objectively. They can turn around a poor negotiation and lead it to find the best alternatives to the negotiated agreement. In addition, they also know their limits and when to walk away from a negotiation. Principled negotiators have a win-win attitude–and this is how they approach every negotiation.

The underlying key to effective negotiation is beyond technical skills. In project management, what's most important are soft skills–skills that can't be taught in formal classrooms. Persuasiveness, negotiations skills, conflict resolution skills, facilitation skills, and "people" skills are just some soft skills that will direct you toward the success of your project as the leader. In some cases, there are individuals born as natural negotiators. They have the innate talent to find ways to get what they want from other people. For some, however, it takes extra effort to make a successful negotiation. In this section, we'll list some items that can help you improve your negotiating skills.

Key negotiation skills include:

Communication skills
Listening skills
Emotional control and regulation
Adapt, sense and control non-verbal communication cues
Goal setting and identifying limitations

Take a moment to reflect on the last time you had to negotiate for your project. How well did you communicate to your co-negotiator what it is that you needed and why you needed it? Did they understand your goals? What was their offer? Did they provide a reasonable proposal? Did you feel pressured into accepting their offer or were you calm and collected throughout the entire ordeal? Did you sense if they were using hard negotiating styles to manipulate you into a poor bargain? Were you able to meet your goals or did you lower your limits to close the deal?

Negotiation can be art; it can also be intense and emotional. Consider the story of Robert Slade and his transition into the world of project management.

If there's one thing Robert Slade knows, it's that everyone has their price. He was a police negotiator, and damn near one of the best. He loved the thrill of it all – the exhilaration of a head-to-head of two minds not willing to back down. A thrill that made the blood rush as he tried to push down the thoughts at the back of his mind; "What if I call it wrong with so much at stake? How can I keep him distracted for enough time? Did I leave the oven on at home again?" He would arrive at the crime scene and the rush would hit again with a sweat-inducing hint of nausea. Or maybe that was from the deep-dish pizza he blitzed at home before he got the call. He would wonder: "Did I even turn the oven on at all?" He was passed the phone from the stern-browned sergeant with a confident nod of the head, then lick his lips, put the receiver to his ear, and say: "My name is Robert Slade, and I'm here to help you."

But those days were over. The precinct's budgets were cut and after much deliberation, Robert was offered redundancy. With a heavy heart, he handed in his badge. A month later, he got a job in OpenEnterprise's head office as a project manager. It wasn't what he wanted, but at least he still got to wear a badge – a name badge. He looked down at it and noticed the waist-length tie he was still unaccustomed to wearing was gently floating in his whiskey-on-the-rocks. He made a mental note to suck it out later. This was the night after his first day in the new job.

He went to bed, unsure he'd made the right decision, and he thought again of taking his friend's offer of a security job at a club – more thrilling, certainly, but the money... Everyone has their price.

The next day, everything changed.

He walked into the briefing room for the morning meeting to hear about his project, nervously fidgeting with his tie to wring out any residual droplets. As he sat down, he glanced up at the whiteboard at the end of the room and something arrested his attention. On the board was a tree diagram of Post-It notes connected with arrows, detailing the process of the planned move to upscale their office location, right from 'Identify a suitable location,' to 'Open for business!' At once, his mind flooded with memories from the precinct. They too used the same method for planning their hostage negotiation strategies, and although those were grittier (most commonly ending with 'Zero casualties!') Robert saw the same process of a successful action being put into place through careful planning and accounting for the dangers of a misjudged prediction.

There were several jobs to be considered to make the plan a success, and he had to find the right person for the task. This was something he was well accustomed to, and he always assigned the best. He thought of his A-team from the precinct, the team that carried him through his most successful negotiations…

For firepower he could always trust Two-Trigger Tony; the man who could shoot twice as fast as any other member of the force. For background research on the suspect, it had to be Sarah 'The Psychic' Higgins, capable of accurately predicting a suspect's behavior with only a handful of notes and his driver Jett, always able to get him to the scene in pole position.

But this project was an altogether different beast, and he'd need a different type of team to come out on top here. Over the next few days, he met and organized the team that would work under him, although he didn't anticipate he'd need his negotiation skills to get them all totally on-board.

First and foremost, he needed a number-cruncher to deal with the figures since money was the firepower of business. He picked the sharp, young Rachael straight out of college with a degree in Finance and a blazing hair of red. Her mind worked fast, but too fast for her own good, and she sat in front of a computer screen for so long. Robert configured her table and borrowed a treadmill off an old friend to give her a stand-up desk, and with a couple packets of Gatorade set to her side; she was happy to get crunching. For a researcher on the other businesses they'd be dealing with, he chose the tech-savvy Zach, a man who could be seen at any given moment keeping track of twenty open tabs, and able to pull out information from the unlikeliest of sources. Zach was competent but frustrated with the old technology of the computers and the inconsistent firewall. Robert gave Zach a company phone (if the situation required it) as long as he promised not to visit his favorite online forums outside of lunch breaks, and Zach happily dual-wielded the phone and mouse to research at a breakneck speed. Lastly, he needed a landline-operator to get important calls to him immediately. Melissa was the obvious choice, fresh out of an HR job for a company that employed upwards of 600 people. This was Robert's toughest task, for she severely disliked Zach and his constant reminders to her that her passwords weren't strong enough. So he took his team out for dinner one night and lubricated conversation with a couple drinks, and Zach and Melissa bonded over the screen of a phone as they watched countless videos of cats.

Two weeks later, it was hard to believe the man who managed the project was the same one who had started with a lost expression on his face and a smelly tie on his chest. His results were lightning fast and always within budget, and the adoption of his negotiation skills was well utilized. Whispers floated in the office regarding Robert, and the water cooler talk lingered on after the inevitable mention of his name, a lingering that frequently required a secondary twizzling of the nozzle for a re-filling of their cups. The well-hydrated workers would hold off their necessity for lavatory relief whenever Robert was seen wielding his weapon of choice – the phone, and a hush would fall over the office as they listened in to the master at work. His team had set him up with all the info and logistics, and he then delivered the goods.

On an ordinary day, he could negotiate upwards of six comprehensive deals with his trusty team behind him. But this was no ordinary day. This was the big one. This was the day Robert had to negotiate with William Crowe, the proprietor of 30% of the entire office spaces in the postcode area and was infamous for being tighter than the shoelaces on Little Lee's ridiculously oversized loafers. Everything was set up for the move. Robert had already procured all the furniture at a knock-off price after he calmly trounced the nervous, young intern desperate for their first sale. He'd purchased all the fittings at a reasonable bargain from a worthier adversary – a wary woman with an icy demeanor Robert was only able to melt with a passing comment about his dog. Seizing his opportunity, he won her over with a sob story about his childhood puppy and a promise for a personal charitable contribution to a local kennel. All they needed now was the actual building. But that Crowe owned building, and he was the toughest bird to make squawk and everyone there knew it.

The conversation that followed tested Robert to his limits, rivaling even his toughest police negotiations and his team had to pull out every trick in the book. Rachael got him the price margin he could work within, Zach got all the info on Crowe's recent sales, and Melissa kept his other communications at bay but still on the hook.

Crowe stated his price with an audible exclamation mark (Robert pictured it as a question mark.) In police negotiations, this was the demand for the helicopter. They never get the helicopter. Rachael held up a relevant note to Robert and he deflected and maneuvered the conversation into safer territory; he mentioned the channeling of the bulk of the company money into the upcoming Christmas marketing campaign, a subtle plea for some leeway. Crowe scoffed, stating: "I may have a big, grey beard but I'm no Santa Claus. I don't give things away for free."

The conversation went on for forty minutes straight, a period of time that felt even longer for the bladder-bursting eavesdroppers, and it was later claimed by Zach that he even saw a slight dribble down the front of Little Lee's ill-fitting pants. Crowe refused to budge, and every light on Melissa's phone was bleeping. She worked her way through them in turn, employing all the sweetness in her voice she could muster. But Robert could feel the deal slipping between his fingers.

All of a sudden, Zach rushed up to him and held the company phone up to his face – there was a news article he had uncovered from an unlisted but verified source. Robert looked at it, smiled, and leaned back in his chair.

"I know about the lawsuit," he coolly revealed. Crowe was silent save for the sound of heavy breathing and a slightly dry croak. Robert was referring to the recent disaster for Crowe's company following a sale they made for a building that was turned into a phone shop. A zit-ridden young man was displaying to a customer the crystal-clear resolution on the new R7 when a slat of roofing dislodged and rapidly descended onto the back of his moppy head. The mishap was incidentally immortalized by the young man in a fortuitously well-timed selfie. Crowe's company took a big hit and they needed quick cash injections to fund the PR recovery. Robert listened to the heavy breathing a moment longer and then gently whispered: "Come on Crowe, give me something to work with here. It's getting late; we both want to get back to our families."

Five minutes later Robert emerged from his desk with a grin beaming on his face, and the office was filled with the sounds of high-fives and toilet flushing.

The next day a call came through to the office. It was Police Chief Barrington, and he wanted to talk to Robert.

"I heard about your negotiation with Crowe. All the boys in the precinct are proud of you for sticking it to the big guy, Rob."

"Everyone has their price," replied Robert. Barrington went on: "But that's not what I'm ringing about. Deputy McNamara handed in his notice this morning. A space has opened up. What do you say? Want to come home?"

Robert stood, the phone at his ear, and looked around the office at his team diligently working away at their own tasks, setting up for a smooth and easy move into the new building, and he felt a profound sense of satisfaction of everything being in its right place.

"I'm already there," answered Robert. He noticed another call coming through. "Can you hold a minute Chief?" He pressed the button to receive the call. "My name is Robert Slade, and I'm here to help you."

As a project manager, you must be a good negotiator to be able to secure whatever your project needs. Having adept negotiation skills puts you in a position of authority among other project managers. It also gives you an edge in access to shared resources. Having the right people-friendly persuasiveness is beneficial when managing multicultural project teams and global stakeholders. Moreover, good negotiators can build good networks and relationships with suppliers, partners, and customers.

The Negotiation Process can be broken down into a systematic process with the following phases:

Phase 1: Pre-Negotiation

Similar to all processes we have discussed so far in this book, the first phase of the negotiation process is the planning. Begin by defining the problem, whether you need a budget increase, additional manpower, or a change in system, and then decide on a solution to identify what you will need to negotiate for. Do your research and gather as much information as possible about the resources you aim to gain in the negotiation and identify the other parties involved in the process. In this step, know the people you are going to be negotiating with, identify their negotiating styles, and plan your strategies and approach accordingly by starting to build relationships with them, if you haven't established one already. Understand the motivators and opinions of affected stakeholders.

Set your desired goals and ensure that your criteria for an acceptable agreement are aligned with the needs of your project. Make sure you are fully aware of the value of what you're negotiating for to avoid making poor bargains and decisions. Be clear about your highest goal and your walk-away position. Your highest goal is the ideal value you aim to get from the negotiation whereas the walk-away position is the lowest threshold where you will close the deal without coming to an agreement. Conduct risk and opportunity assessments and gauge the possible impact of each option. Try to imagine all possible worst-case scenarios and think of plans for resolutions. Plot your timelines and consider timing and conditions, such as the urgency of the negotiation and the availability of the other parties involved. Arrange for a conducive negotiation in an area that is non-threatening and culturally appropriate. Ensure that attendees and participants will be comfortable and relaxed.

Phase 2: Negotiation Meeting / Engaging

The actual negotiation process begins upon engaging the parties involved and ends when they arrive at the mutually acceptable agreements.

Step 1: Discussing

The second phase is the beginning of the communication among the parties within the negotiating setting. Project managers often take the lead in discussing the nature of the negotiation, identifying the key issues, and helping the parties involved understand the rationale of the negotiation. In this step, you must be clear with your goals. Unless you clarify what, it is that you want from the negotiation, you put yourself at risk of settling for a bad deal. At the same time, this is your opportunity to probe the motivations of the other party. Don't just seek to understand what they want but explore further to determine why they want it in the first place. Some basic idea of what each party will want to talk about here is, "Here's what I have" and "Here's what I don't have."

Step 2: Proposing

When the details have been laid out and all parties have gained an understanding of the issues, the project manager or the facilitator of the negotiation present their proposal. At this point, you open the discussion to answer, "Where can we go from here?"

Step 3: Bargaining

At this step, collaborate with the other parties to generate and evaluate other optional trade-offs. Open the discussion to alternative exchanges that will meet the needs and goals of all parties. You might want to lead with the question, "What else can we do about this?"

Step 4: Agreement

After bargaining, parties are expected to select and arrive at a mutually acceptable joint agreement. Action plans and timelines are also developed and settled.

Next steps:

Step 1: Documentation

As a project manager, ensure that the discussions and agreements that transpired in the negotiation are properly documented. All parties concerned must be furnished with copies to make sure that everyone's in the loop and informed of the arrangements.

Step 2: Monitoring

Monitoring may be necessary to assure that the action plans are implemented and the agreements from the negotiations are put into effect.

Step 3: Evaluation and Analysis

Evaluate the effectiveness of the entire negotiation process. Assess how effective the planning and outcomes were and identify areas for improvement. Note any significant events that may be used as relevant information in future discussions.

It's not just important to close the negotiation; one critical element in being a good negotiator is knowing what a successful negotiation looks like. In the previous sections, we talked about how win-win negotiations are ideal because the end goal is to arrive at a mutually beneficial decision where all parties win and walk away happily. A successful negotiation is not a scenario where all parties get exactly what they want, but the final agreement provides them with what they need, plus you can also make incremental gains that can improve your position in future negotiations. A successful negotiation is a win-win negotiation. As you progress as a negotiator for your projects, you will learn that win-lose negotiations will result in lose-lose outcomes in the long run. They can hurt your chances of winning in future negotiations and deals. It also creates negative competitive among other parties and can cause unnecessary conflict. In win-win negotiations, you not only get a good bargain that meets your needs, but you also build good networks with the people you are negotiating with. Again, the secret is to win with a win-win attitude.

Negotiations can be intimidating and overwhelming. It's important to enter any negotiation, no matter big or small, prepared and knowledgeable. The following are some common mistakes that leaders make when negotiating:

Failing to prepare

Don't enter a negotiation without sufficient knowledge of your goals, the other party's goals and key motivators. You will easily be caught off guard and may be cornered into settling for a poor deal. Even when you are an experienced negotiator, don't overlook the importance of practice and preparation.

Proposing unreasonable offers

The goal in negotiations is to arrive at an agreeable solution for all parties. Don't make the mistake of giving unfair or impractical proposals. Some negotiators are prone to make unnecessary compromises in their bargain just to gain approval from other parties. Be smart about your offers. This will not only give you an edge in the negotiation itself, but you will also gain the respect of the people you're negotiating with.

Don't be afraid of using "time outs" when negotiations have become uncertain.

"Time outs" and postponements are available options for negotiators who feel they are being rushed into a decision. Don't make the mistake of being pressured into settling for an unsatisfactory agreement because of time constraints. Additionally, don't enter negotiations with the aim to leave at the earliest opportunity. Some negotiators end up with lousy deals because they rushing into closing negotiations.

Settling for less than your required goals

Never lose sight of your targets. In negotiations, stay firm with your goals and lowest walk-away point. Not all negotiations need to end at an agreement, especially when you will be at the losing end of a win-lose negotiation.

Failing to maintain composure

Because negotiations can be a tricky ordeal, failing to prepare can make you uncomfortable when entering the process. Always walk into a negotiation with the end in mind. Know your goals and be confident with your offer. Many negotiators fail because they try to get too much from the negotiation.

As mentioned, project managers will be expected to use negotiating skills in every step of the project and with everyone involved in the project. There are negotiations in your regular engagements as project managers that don't have a major impact on the project itself–it's just part of the project management cycle and passes by without being identified as an actual negotiation.

But there are also negotiations that are critical to the project's needs and therefore must be handled proficiently. In these kinds of negotiation, we'll mostly find project stakeholders involved, geared with their goal to meet their different interests. Project managers negotiate on resources, budget, time frames, and scope, to name a few. Technical officers may negotiate on the technical components. Business analysts negotiate on the specifics of the product. Executives negotiate for more ROI.

The nature of your negotiation will also vary depending on where you are in the project cycle. In the planning phase, you will need to set the right balance in time frames, costing, quality, and scope with all stakeholders. Furthermore, contracts will need to be arranged, you will have to present to the stakeholders, and have all of them come to terms with the full project plan. As the wheels of the project begin to turn, you may need to negotiate with service providers, vendors, and other line managers or department heads for mobilization and procurement. Going along further into the project, you will encounter conflicts and potential risks where you will need to negotiate solutions. As discussed in the previous chapter, you will also experience change requests that may need to be negotiated to maintain the integrity of your project. Other typical issues that may be negotiated during the project life cycle are changes in the project plan, contract terms and conditions, project team assignments, roles, and responsibilities, and other project resources.

Good negotiation skills go hand in hand with good communication skills. Communication is the main key that will ignite the engine to drive the negotiation process. To be an effective negotiator, you should also be aware of the communication models commonly used in a negotiation process.

Arrow model

The arrow model is a one-way communication approach where a message is sent from a sender to a receiver without the need for feedback. In this model, there is no way to confirm if the message has been received and understood.

Circuit model

The circuit model is like the arrow model, but the receiver sends feedback to acknowledge receipt and understanding of the message. Oftentimes, feedback that confirms receipt of the message is taken as an acceptance and agreement to the proposed terms of the negotiation.

Dance model

In the dance model, communication is a two-way approach where messages flow back and forth and both ends in the communication line are both senders and receivers simultaneously. In negotiations, parties commonly follow the dance model so each party has the opportunity to present, listen, and respond to persuade the other.

Here are additional tips that you can take into practice to be a highly skilled negotiator:

Do your research

If you don't know whom you're dealing with, you're bound to make mistakes. Gather as much information you can about the other parties. Don't be hesitant to ask questions and find out what their motivations are, whom they report to, what timelines they're following, if they have previously engaged in negotiations before, and what possible alternative solutions they would be willing to accept. You can use this information in the bargaining step to make the most out of the negotiation process for both of you.

Be mindful also to consider any relevant social or cultural conventions when you are planning to negotiate with people from different cultures. Different organizations and teams from different areas may have different ways of working. It will help you to know their norms and standards when negotiating with other people. When people feel respected, they feel valued. Respecting other people's cultures will go a long way in helping you achieve a successful negotiation.

Come prepared

Never enter a negotiation without enough preparation. Condition yourself to have the proper mindset by practicing, no matter how many times you have done bargaining and closed deals before.

Bring all the relevant knowledge you've gathered from your prior investigations. Prepare to give counter-proposals and strengthen your position by presenting the value of your bargaining chips.

Preparing yourself also means preparing your team. When their involvement is necessary, include them in the loop and inform them about the situation to get their feedback and recommendations. Share with them your plans so in case unexpected circumstances arise, you won't need to worry about backup plans and communication procedures.

Know the market rates of what you want and how much it costs. Be prepared to enter negotiations with a clear understanding of what the business costs are.

Use your timeouts

Don't rush the process. Take your time. If you feel that the current meeting will not lead you and the other party towards a productive settlement, don't hesitate to take a time-out and reschedule.

Make the negotiating circle small

If you have the authority to control the number of people involved in the negotiation process, minimize the number of individuals who will represent each party. It will help to keep the circle small and free from negative parties who are not essential in the negotiation and decision-making.

Be transparent

When presenting during negotiations, be honest and transparent. Deception does not belong in professional negotiations. Some individuals are keen on using deception to land deals; they would hide their actual budget or give false data about their available resources and requirements, just to manipulate the proceedings of the negotiation and place themselves at an advantage. In the same light, it's also easy to get pressured into decreasing your actual demands to gain a positive impression from your co-negotiators. While twisting the truth can have immediate visible benefits and being consistently truthful may feel like putting yourself in a vulnerable position, in the long run, your integrity and credibility as project manager will suffer. Understand the potential long-term consequences you may cause to yourself and your project if you were be caught in a lie, you'd be known for being manipulative to win in negotiations. It will be more difficult to establish trusting relationships with stakeholders and other partners.

We don't suggest playing all your cards at once or putting all your aces on the table immediately. Rather, in negotiations, what's most important is to be open about your goals and intentions. Be sincere in understanding the other parties involved and in seeking the best possible outcomes for everyone.

In most negotiations, all parties are there because they need something. You can address the elephant in the room more quickly if you begin by breaking the ice and opening the discussion for a straightforward dialogue. After presenting the nature of the negotiation, you can state your offer: (1) Here's what I have, and (2) Here's what I don't have. Then initiate a flow of exchange by asking: Where do we go from here?

Be fair with your authority

Being the leader of a project gives you an edge in some negotiation processes. Don't underestimate your power. To speed up a negotiation with a decision-maker, you can deal with the other party directly to arrive at an agreement quickly. However, in exchanges where you are the decision-maker, sometimes its valuable to have someone negotiate on your behalf. Take the backseat and enable others to facilitate the bargaining so you can review the proposals objectively and prepare better counter proposals.

Always be reasonable

Negotiations can be tricky, and you can expect other parties to pull off tactics to gain more in the exchange. It can be easy to fall into this trap, but you must be mindful to stand firm with your limits. Be reasonable with your own inputs and with the bargains you will be willing to entertain and accept. If the proposals are below the value of what you have to offer, negotiate with due diligence and with your limits clear and firm. Don't give in to hardcore intimidation tactics and lower what you're willing to accept in the exchange. Some of these tactics could be used against you: threat (If you don't do this, we'll cut your entire budget), bribery (If you agree to this, we'll vouch for you for the promotion you're applying for), or a fake appeal to trust (Don't you trust that we can land that contract with the new client?). Watch out for these hard communication styles and be careful in dealing with unreasonable negotiators. Don't hesitate to counter their proposal with questions and with the information you have gathered from your prior research.

Remember, the goal of the negotiation is to get what you want at a reasonable cost, nothing less.

Learn when to walk away

This next point goes hand in hand with the previous tip. Knowing your limits will help you determine whether to continue in presenting counter-proposals or walk away.

Be a force of positivity

In the negotiation process, being positive will help make your job as a project manager easier. By bringing in a positive attitude to the negotiating table, you can create a positive atmosphere where people may be keener to cooperate and aim for equally favorable outcomes for all parties involved. Exhibiting positivity towards your stakeholders also helps build confidence and trust that will make them more likely to support your project and provide what you need to get things done efficiently.

People are more likely to compromise with people they like. Having a pleasing and positive personality will not just earn you a vote in Mr. and Ms. Congeniality but it will also help you win in negotiations.

This bears repeating:
Always aim for the win-win

Win-win outcomes not only get you desirable outcomes, but it will also help your preserve good relationships with the other parties, giving you better chances for increment gains in continuous exchanges with them.

Try to look at the other parties as allies, not as competitors. Acknowledge that in the negotiation process, while each party may have different concerns, each one has the ability to help each other and that all parties can win something from the discussion. Establish rapport and set common goals with them to build an equal level playing ground. Seek to understand their beliefs, motivations, and goals and collaborate with them to analyze potential outcomes and risks and to identify win-win alternatives. Don't involve personal issues and focus on the goals at hand.

Oftentimes, a win-lose ending leads to lose-lose outcomes. Win-lose negotiations result in one or more parties walking away defeated. This can be bad for your project and for you as the project manager. Your relationships with stakeholders, vendors, and suppliers, and other project leads, and officers are vital in

Walk in the other negotiator's shoes

Negotiators will be coming to the table with various proposal and demands. Train yourself to be empathetic and understand where their motivations are coming from. Thinking from their perspective will help you gain better insight and determine the threshold of their limits, so you can come up with counter-proposals you can bargain with to get the best deal for both of you.

Take your time

If you go into a negotiation with your mind set on closing a deal the soonest time possible, you're bound to make poor decisions and end up in the losing side of the win-lose negotiation. Take your time to build rapport with the other person. Get their feedback and show that you are sincere with your intentions in arriving at a mutually agreeable resolution that will be beneficial to both of you. Probe and ask questions. When you are asked a question, don't hesitate to answer with another question. Invite the other party to give their recommendations. Merge your inputs together and invest enough time in conducting the first stage of the integrative approach, which is increasing the total value of the resources being negotiated.

Being patient will take you a long way in negotiations. It enables you to have better control and propose deals that are more rational. Rushing into the negotiation process can lead to faulty openings and poor relations with the other parties involved. Walking the negotiation process quickly may give the other party the advantage of pressuring you into accepting less than what you had originally bargained for. When you need extra time to think, ask questions and probe further to gain better insights into the situation. Don't be hesitant to consider interim options or postponing making a final decision. If the additional needed information is required, or you're unable to come to a desirable outcome, buy yourself some time to recollect and set another time to negotiate.

Mind your timelines

Double check the time frame of your project and how negotiation can affect this. Though it's recommended that you give major negotiations enough time to arrive at a successful outcome, you don't want to be pressed against a deadline and hasten the decision-making.

Increase your E.Q.

As we mentioned, the more important skills in negotiations are soft skills, including how you handle emotions—yours and the other persons. Some people will attempt to persuade by appealing to the human factor and involve emotions in the discussions, especially in more challenging cases. Be wary of both verbal and non-verbal cues and keep your eyes open for emotional triggers. Remain calm and defuse elevated emotions by extending your patience, empathizing, and acknowledging how that other party feels. When the other party is expressively angry, allow the person to vent while subtly probing for the reasons. Or, when the other party showers you with false flattery to talk you into saying yes to their proposals, focus on your goals and don't be swayed. Avoid giving emotional responses to forceful and argumentative rebuttals. In case the discussion becomes excessively heated, don't allow emotions to further escalate. Suggest a timeout or to postpone the decision-making at a time when conditions are better.

Know your own emotional "buttons" too and be aware of your weaknesses. Do you remember the last time you felt pressured and manipulated? Whom were you dealing with? What triggered you? What subjects were you discussing? How did you react? In case it happens again, how will you react differently to arrive at a more ideal outcome? Keep in mind that the same way you will attempt to understand the other party; they will also be looking to identify you. Being self-aware will help you avoid being sidetracked in case anyone begins to press your hot buttons. Pre-identify techniques that work for you, so you can remain calm and impartial in any situation.

Know the ropes of bargaining

If possible, let the other parties go first when presenting proposals. Knowing what they're offering will give you the opportunity to adjust in your counter-offer and will give you an advantage in the bargaining process. Expect that their offer will not be the best and it won't be their final either. Don't accept the initial offer immediately. Prepare your own proposal and set it at maximum. Don't be afraid to aim high because this will increase your playing field and give you enough space to adjust until you reach the level of comfortability to close a deal.

Keep in mind that often, you will not share the same underlying interests, motivations, or limitations with the other party. The stakes look different from where either of you is standing. From this perspective, you can increase the total value of the resources being negotiated by keeping your eyes open for things that are of low cost to the one and of high value to the other. Remember, your goal is not a winner-takes-all outcome; you want to bargain well enough to maximize the resources available from both parties and allocate this, so everyone gets a good deal and meets their needs.

Stir in some creativity in the process

Being a good negotiator requires you to be quick and creative on your feet. Creativity is a handy skill when coming up with innovative alternatives as compared to being limited by the restrained processes and guidelines in negotiations. Have an open mind and think outside the box to find solutions that will serve all parties well. Let your imagination run wild and seek out alternatives. This helps speed up decision-making, and it increases your appeal and credibility in executive negotiations. Just be mindful not to make poor hastened decisions.

Consider the communication models

If you don't know how to effectively communicate what you need, you won't be able to achieve what you want. Make sure you have a clear picture of whom you're negotiating with and know their culture and preferred communication styles.

Remember that these are just tips on how to manage negotiations. At the end of the day, the idea is to find your personal strategy, one that you are comfortable with. Know the basics, adhere to the system, but don't be afraid to experiment further to find innovative solutions and approaches that can help you consistently land a win-win agreement for you and for other parties involved. The best way to win in a negotiation is to go in with a win-win attitude. Remember, the goal is to find a common ground where everyone can find the best outcome.

CHAPTER 6 DELEGATING

"The first rule of management is delegation. Don't try and do everything yourself because you can't."
-Anthea Turner

Management is all about getting things done through people. Delegation is all about assigning responsibilities to other people. In other words, when you delegate, you turn over a task to another person or give someone else a job to do.

It's not uncommon for leaders to hesitate when delegating their own tasks. Naturally, they may feel uneasy entrusting a task to someone else, especially when they know they are highly skilled and competent to deliver the best outcomes. They might worry that the result may not be as good as it could be if they do it themselves, that deadlines might not be met, and that their subordinates might not be able to collaborate effectively with others.

This mindset, however, not only hinders leaders from allocating higher responsibilities among their teams but also from practicing effective people management. Delegation goes hand in hand with project management. Having a project team with several members focusing on one or two tasks each is more efficient and more productive than having only one person juggle multiple tasks at once. No one person can be everything to a project– even the project leader. The success of your project relies on the collaborative efforts of your team. The reason why the first point of discussion in wrangling squirrels is how to build an effective team is that your team will determine the success of your project. But having the right people on board is just the first step–you have the get them doing the right things as well. It doesn't just stop at appointing people for their specific roles and responsibilities in the project, but it also means sharing higher functions among your team through effective delegation. Remember, to be able to get more work done, you need more people doing the work.

With that in mind, take a look at the brief story of Karen Roberts and how she learned the value of effective delegation.

The day before November 22 is always the busiest in the life of Karen Roberts, Fresh Foods department manager at Greenway Supermarket. Customers flood the shop floor for their Thanksgiving Day necessities. Some come to raid the shelves and fill their trolleys with last-minute vegetables, trimmings, and alcohol; others collect their turkeys, pre-ordered well in advance, ready for roasting the next afternoon— a task which awaited Karen if she'd successfully make it through the day. It's a time of the year in which supermarket workers give little thanks for, and this was to be the busiest in Karen's twenty-five-year-long career to date.

Despite Greenway's remaining open on Thanksgiving, Karen always made sure that she had the day booked a holiday, which only added to the stress of that manic Wednesday. Making sure that everything was in place for her absence the next day added to the list of tasks she'd have to navigate and so meant cramming as many tasks into the working day as possible.

Karen checked the clock on her car's dashboard; it read 6:45AM. The store's car park was nearly empty. Dispersed sporadically were the automobiles of some night-shift workers, lit by the artificial light from street lamps. The sun would remain in hiding for a few hours yet, a good thing Karen thought, well aware of the chaos, which would ensue once it did eventually rise and draw the shoppers from their beds and through Greenway's double-doors. The first job of the morning was the problematic task of wheeling out the extra shelving, a necessity for the obscene amount of vegetables to be placed on the daily delivery. The problem didn't lay in the wheeling of the units but instead in locating their whereabouts. Most likely hidden away in some back room of the warehouse and no doubt obscured further from sight by heaps of other seasonal clutter, pinpointing their exact location would be a lottery. A few other members of Fresh would be starting at seven but Karen needed them to get everything set up for the upcoming delivery, and so she began her game of hiding and seek alone.

Wrangling Squirrels

The warehouse was large, and a few night workers were huddled in one corner looking distinctly idle. When they caught sight of Karen heading in their direction you could almost see the panic in their eyes as they shuffled about trying to look busy. "Have any of you seen the additional shelving units up here?" She asked nobody and everybody. There were a few unhelpful murmurs before one of the senior members of the gang gave any kind of meaningful response. "Think they're in with the pallets. We could help you look if you like." You could see the frowns appear on the rest of the faces, they knew they were clocking out in ten minutes and there was no guessing how much clutter might need shifting to clear the debris. "You've been helpful enough," Karen replied, reluctant to prolong the shift of the already weary-eyed night owls. If in twenty-five years of work, Karen had garnered a reputation for anything it was this: her ability to stand firmly on her own two feet; a dignified reluctance to ask colleagues for help with work she knew she was perfectly capable of completing herself. It was at times such as now when she approached the closet door and saw the sheer number of wooden pallets heaped in front of the shelves; this commendable characteristic seemed to be as much a curse as it was a blessing. The door had a 'DO NOT SHUT' sign taped on it, which made Karen chuckle as the overflowing contents of the room apparently made this an impossibility.

An hour and a half of heavy lifting later and most shelving units were stacked neatly outside the storeroom door, a dark, dingy space better described as a cave than a 'room'. The process had taken longer than she might have liked as her work phone had been steadily ringing with customer turkey collections. Her various trips to the meat fridge and down to the shop floor were a nuisance but it was a job she was reluctant to delegate to one of her fresh colleagues - the click-and-collect turkey service was the crown jewel in Greenway's Thanksgiving trading and Karen knew the importance of delivering a flawless service. As she lugged the final shelving unit onto the warehouse floor. Karen felt warmed by that addictive sensation of satisfaction that came with completing such an arduous task by herself, a reminder of why she consistently went "above and beyond" as her store manager had once put it in a colleague review meeting. The moment was cut short though as her phone began to ring again, another turkey order no doubt. She reached in her pocket but felt nothing apart from her extended daily checklist, which she'd compiled the night before. The tone was beginning to echo and must have fallen out of her pocket in the 'cave.' As she retreated into the darkness of the now perfectly tidy storeroom, she heard a resounding 'clunk' from behind her.

The phone call was indeed another turkey collection. However, that was now completely irrelevant. The 'clunking' noise which sounded behind Karen as she reached for her phone was the sound of her day turning to complete ruin. It was no longer a cave but instead a cell, to which she was a prisoner. The door handle, which she now noticed for the first time, was completely knackered— accounting for the oversized 'DO NOT SHUT' sign stuck to the other side. She quickly typed 301 into her phone and was promptly greeted by Sasha from checkouts: "Customer services, how can I help you?" Karen quickly explained her situation to the young checkout boy and moments later, she heard a loud bang on the door. "Hello, anybody in there?" It was Trevor, the store's maintenance guy. "It's me, Karen, I'm locked in here!" she said with real urgency. There was a brief silence. "Do you realize there's a big sign with "DO NOT SHUT" stuck on the door, Karen?" She didn't have time for this. "Yes! I didn't mean to shut it, Trevor." Another silence ensued. "I've been meaning to fix that door for a while but couldn't get inside with all that junk in there… Oh, someone's cleaned it all up. They should have told me, I could've fixed the door."

Karen pulled her checklist from her pocket and used her phone's flashlight to illuminate its contents. She read:

- Find additional shelving units

- Assemble additional shelving units

- Unload delivery

- Stay on top of turkey collections

- Redress soups

- Refrigerator temperature checks

- GO HOME AND PREP TURKEY

She drew a line through the first item on the list and desperately scanned the rest for anything else she might be able to discard. No luck. Karen's usual method of management generally went something like this: Figure out exactly what needs doing, devise a list of all these things, check and see who's working shift that day, ignore the previous step and physically do EVERYTHING yourself as there will be nobody else to blame if something goes wrong. Her current predicament, however, meant that she was forced into doing the one thing she detested the most: relying on her team to do the jobs they're paid to do without any major or potentially disastrous hiccups. Below the list of tasks, she jotted down the names of the five fresh colleagues she knew would be milling around downstairs, most probably with their hands in their pockets pondering the whereabouts of their trusted department manager: Gary, Jeremy, Anne, Tom, and Hayley. She would match each of these names with one of the tasks above, and then pray that by some Thanksgiving Day miracle, she wouldn't have to work through the night to clear up their mess.

Assemble additional shelving units. A relatively easy task once you have a basic understanding of how each unit attaches to the next. Probably best suited for somebody who's good with their hands and relatively practical, Karen thought. She remembered that Jeremy had last year surprised her with his assembling of all the cardboard Thanksgiving decorations the store had been sent from head office, the same cardboard which Karen had cut her finger on when attempting herself. She drew a line from his name.

Unload delivery: She checked the time on her phone, there were approximately fifteen minutes until the lorry would be backing up downstairs, eager to empty its contents and quickly scoot off to its next stop. Speed was key here. Who would be able to get the produce off the lorry and into the fridges ASAP without a potato spilled or squash smashed? Well, that would be Tom, she thought. Despite his flaws, and there were many, he has a brilliant skill for whizzing through any task which might prevent him from clocking out as much as one minute past his allotted time. If he channeled that intensity now it would be done in record time, she added a side note: 'Tell him he can leave an hour early if it's completed before 10AM.'

Stay on top of Turkey collections: Probably one of the most stressful tasks of the day and one requiring great diligence. Karen thought back to last year's turkey service and remembered the foul look on the face of one customer to whom she'd delivered the wrong fowl. Only Anne could be trusted with this, and now that she thought about it, it was Anne who had taken over the service last year after Karen had made a proverbial turkey of it.

Redress Soups: Greenway's seasonal delivery of 'Potato, Leek and Bacon Soup' was a particularly big one this year. Karen wanted it front, middle, and center of the display to draw in as many wandering eyes as she could to shift the lot. This had Hayley written all over it, as she would frequently decorate the staff canteen with picturesque floral arrangements that always captured the attention of any worker who'd just walked through the doors.

Refrigerator temperature checks: With only Gary left empty-handed, Karen was forced into assigning him what was, on paper, the easiest job of the day: Walking around the aisles and poking an electrical thermometer right where the sun don't shine – at the very back of the shelving behind the rows of food. The fridges needed to be tested to make sure they were operating within the required temperature limit. If they were over by so much as one degree, they'd have to be emptied immediately before the food was rendered unsellable. An easy job, sure, but still important.

Karen grabbed her phone and typed in 301. "Customer services, how can I help you?" Sasha replied in that monotone voice again. "Sasha, it's Karen. I've got some instructions for you to pass on for me. Grab a pen and paper." The list was long and precise; the least Karen could do now was to relay to her team exactly what needed doing, and by whom, and by that time. It was about five minutes before Sasha finally managed to get a word in himself. "Oh, Karen, bad news about Trevor by the way, he said it's going to take him at least three…" the line abruptly cut out. Karen pulled the phone from her ear and started frantically tapping buttons. Nothing happened. The battery had died. And with that so did Karen's faint hopes of a happy Thanksgiving.

The storeroom turned cave, turned prison cell, was truly dark now that Karen's phone had fallen into a deep slumber. And with little else to do Karen decided her best course of action was to follow suit. She propped up a stack of unused advertising hoardings against a wall and unzipped her work fleece, covering herself with it as a makeshift duvet. As she closed her eyes she thought about her family; her kids, her husband; her turkey sat in the fridge at home, waiting to be seasoned, stuffed and strewn up. Then she thought about her expectations for the shop downstairs, and she buried her face into the fleece with terror at the thought of the bumbling collection of people she now had no choice but to put her faith in. The thoughts only disappeared when she passed into a sleep in which she tossed and turned.

She awoke to the sound of a creek and a beam of light shot across her eyes. She squinted up at her radiant savior. It was Trevor, a crowbar in one hand and a half-eaten sandwich in the other. "Sorry, I know I said three hours, but I couldn't find the good spanner, and then what with a lunch break and all..." Karen bolted past him, hurled herself down the stairs three-per-step and flung open the door to the shop floor, expecting to see something or other on fire, and maybe Gary being strangled by a belligerent customer for the second time this year. What she saw made her freeze in her step, and it was nothing she could have ever expected.

Everything was fine. Completely and utterly fine. Better than fine, even. The shop floor was awash with customers happily going about their day, cramming their trolleys with products off the well-filled shelves. Karen walked around her department – the shelving was fitted and stable, the delivery done and dusted, the turkey's in the hands of the rightful owners, the soups decorated and selling fast, and the fridge's blowing out regulatory crisp, cold air. Karen was stunned as she watched her team calmly managing their jobs as the day went on until closing time. Not only did she not need to do everything herself, but also things were better for it. Greenway hit a home run; spectacular sales, great customer feedback, and the only thing wrapped around Gary's neck was his Thanksgiving scarf his Mom got him for the walk home. Karen left the store feeling as if she'd swallowed a big bite of humble pie. But for the main course... It was time for her to get stuffing that turkey.

It was the day before Christmas and the shop floor of Greenway supermarket was packed full of customers. Shoppers were in for their last-minute festive food, booze, and presents. It was typically the second busiest day in the life of Karen Roberts, Fresh Foods department manager. But owing to recent events, she was now a different type of busy. She sat at her seat in 'The Cove' – what used to be known as the 'cave' was now Karen's well-lit office, and from there she delegated to her team what needed to be done throughout the day via her phone whilst she kept up with important matters on her desktop computer; if anyone needed her, they knew the phone number. She had a busy day ahead, but there was one thing that needed to be done first. She pressed 'Print' on the computer, took out the freshly printed sheet, and got the tape ready to stick it on the outside of the door. She stuck it up, and then went back inside. 'DO NOT DISTURB'

A project leader can't be expected to do all the tasks no matter how good he/she is. If you work on your own, there's a limited amount of work you can do in a span of time. Because your work is limited, so is your success.

Here are some signs that you need to work on your delegating skills as project leader:

You are becoming overwhelmed with work. Despite efforts to practice time management or seek out help from others, you are always too busy with work. You haven't finished with one task yet and you're already taking on another one. The job just keeps piling up and it's overwhelming you. This is the first sign that you must start delegating to other people.

You are starting to lose focus on your work. Having too much on your plate can compromise your focus on the more important things in the project. Excessive workloads can be very stressful and can affect your overall productivity. There may be small things that don't necessarily need your attention and can be delegated to other people in your team.

You are not as productive as desired. Having too many tasks can affect your productivity. It divides your attention, time, energy, and other resources, and can compromise your overall productivity.

You are not confident about your team's abilities. You take on all the workload because you don't trust that the others will be able to do them as well you. This is problematic for many reasons. If you're not able to have confidence in your team's abilities, you will always be carrying the burden of the entire workload.

There are a few reasons why leaders don't delegate as much they should. Some have been mentioned in the first part of this chapter but let's talk about them more thoroughly.

- Delegating tasks seems like it's making the work more complicated. It takes more effort to assign the job to someone else and you must explain the guidelines, prepare the instructions, track their progress, and provide feedback and coaching. You'll also have to keep checking how they're doing. It seems easier to just do the job yourself.

- Delegating tasks will make you look lazy. Why would you give the work to someone else if you can do it yourself? Your people will think you are slacking off and passing the responsibility onto them.

- Delegating task will make you look incompetent. If you give a task to someone else in your team and they do it better than you do, you will look inept as the leader.

- Delegating tasks will only compromise the output. You are a project manager for a reason—and that's because you're the best person for the role and for the job. You are the person with the skills and competence to get the work done in the best possible way. There's one best way to get the job right and nobody else can do it as well as you. If the task will be assigned to someone else, the outcome may be compromised.

- Delegating tasks will waste time. If you work on the task yourself, you can complete it faster. Assigning someone else to do it will consume more time and can affect not just your work schedule, but the others' as well. This can cause disruptions in your workflows and timelines.

These may seem valid reasons to opt out of delegating tasks and sometimes they can be. But in the long run, delegating tasks will help you reap benefits that outweigh these challenges. There is nothing discreditable and shameful about entrusting work to someone. When done effectively, delegating tasks can save you and your team time and can significantly increase your productivity and the success of your project.

As a project leader, it's part of your responsibility to get your team involved and challenged. Though it may sound difficult and arduous, you must provide opportunities for them to step outside the comforts of their job and take on bigger responsibilities that will teach them new skills and help them grow professionally. It's also your responsibility to oversee the operations of the project and ensure that the best outcomes are achieved. As project leader, your function is to lead your project team, not to do everything by yourself. If you're unable to give up the tasks that you used to do before you became the project manager, it means you're not doing your job correctly. If you are at a level that enables you to delegate but you are still doing the work yourself, you're failing to make the best use of your position and your time. Remember that as a project manager, your role is to be the manager of the project, not the technician who does the groundwork.

A leader is someone who enables their team. They cultivate a work environment where team members are empowered and results-driven, motivated by their common goals and work interdependently with each other.

The manifestation of a good leader is when their team can function with as much efficiency even in their absence. The good leader manages the least, so to speak. Understanding this is the first step to delegate effectively. Giving people higher responsibilities exposes them to new experiences from which they can learn. If you don't delegate, you may be depriving your team the opportunity to widen their horizons and maximize their potential, especially their leadership skills. Delegating is also a form of mentoring. By allowing them the chance to take on more responsibility, you are honing the future leader in them by building their confidence, strengthening competencies, and empowering them to gain new skills and proficiencies. You are also training them to become self-sufficient team players that you can trust to function and to keep the wheels turning smoothly even without your direct supervision and involvement. Basically, you're preparing them for future projects and future leadership positions.

Consider the following:

- How critical is the task at hand? Is it a task someone else from the team can do or is it paramount that you handle it personally because it may involve highly confidential information? Is there anyone in the team who has the expertise or the authority to complete the task?

- Do you and your team have the time for effective delegation? This includes debriefing, turnover, monitoring, and coaching and rework, if necessary. What are the consequences if the task is not completed in time?

- How crucial is it that the expected outcomes are met with exact precision? What are the possible repercussions if the results are unsatisfactory? How would failure affect other elements in the project?

- Will delegating the task open doors of opportunities of professional growth for others? How can this task help the person you will be delegating this too? Will this be just an additional burden on top of their workload?

With all these factors taken into consideration, you will still not be guaranteed that the task will be completed successfully. It is also important to take account of the persons you will be delegating the task to.

Your team may be resistant at first. You can expect to hear comments such as: "Why is my project manager giving me his job?" "Why am I being asked to do this extra work?" "I'm busy enough already, why am I given the burden of this extra assignment?" "My project manager is slacking off and making other people do his job for him." They may not immediately understand the essence of delegating tasks, especially from your role as the project manager. However, you can avoid this by delegating the right way.

After having decided to delegate a task, you should next deliberate other factors relating to your team members. Don't make the mistake of carelessly giving out assignments without considering the nature of the task and the competence and motivations of the person you will be delegating the task to. This means making sure that when you entrust responsibility to a person, the work is a match or a fit to their professional profile and skills. What existing skills do they already have and what is their expertise? It may backfire on you if you delegate administrative tasks to somebody who specializes in IT. In the same light, giving an entry-level staff member an assignment that involves crucial decision-making may not work out so well either. In situations like this, you'll have to take over when the person fails to deliver, giving you and the person, wasting time and energy. Do you have the time and resource to provide any training needed for them? You must determine how willing the person is to accept added responsibility. What do they want from their current job? What are their long-term goals and how do these align with the task at hand? Are they exhibiting positive attitudes toward their jobs? Are they demonstrating the willingness to accept challenges and to contribute further to the project? They may know what you are asking of them, but they may not be motivated to get it done. In worst-case scenarios, you might have people who are both incapable and unmotivated. These are the kind of people who can't be bothered to go the extra mile. If they can't be shifted into a role where they can maximize their potential and make significant contributions despite engaging them, you might want to reconsider their place in your team. This is one of the reasons why it's important to get the right people in your team—the kind of people who are not only well-suited for the job but have the drive, motivation, and openness to take on bigger responsibilities for their individual and collective growth and development.

Upon identifying your team member, the first thing you need to do is explain the work. Arrange a meeting with the person to discuss the task thoroughly. Start by stating your intentions and begin with the end in mind. Specify the expected outcomes and clearly provide the nature of the task. "I'd like you to take charge of sending the weekly collated progress reports to the rest of the team from now on until the end of the project cycle." Be direct and straightforward with what you're asking. "The report should show our running numbers, laid out in an Excel Worksheet. Attach any relevant documents to back up the data in the email. This should be sent via email every Friday one hour before the end of the shift. Make sure to CC the senior manager." Ask if the person has any clarifications or questions. "Do you have any questions? Do you need me to guide you in creating the template of the report?" If the delegate has done a similar task before, it won't be necessary for you to go into much detail. However, if this will be an entirely new task to her, you may have to be more particular with the details. Establish their controls, limitations, constraints, boundaries, and other necessary information they need to understand the assignment. Help them understand the importance of the task. Explain to them why it's crucial that it must be done efficiently and why they were chosen as the point person for it. Make sure they see this as an opportunity, even as a reward, and not as a punishment.

Open a discussion to listen to their feedback and ask for suggestions they might have to make the process more smooth-sailing for them. "Is this a task you're comfortable with? Are you up for it? Will this disrupt any of your current responsibilities? Do you have any recommendations on how we can do the process?" Lastly, make sure that they know that you are available for any questions or clarifications if they encounter any challenges as the work progresses. Express your support. "If you have any questions, feel free to approach me at any time. Should you encounter any challenge communicating with the rest of the time, let me know. If you need any technical assistance, send me your recommendations and request so I can endorse them to the IT department."

Delegating doesn't mean leaving the entire responsibility to the person you have assigned it to. As the leader, you are still responsible for keeping control of the operations and ensuring that the project plans are carried out successfully. However, as a manager, the last thing you want to do is to micromanage your people. In delegating tasks, you must find the right balance between keeping an eye on their activities and giving them the space to work at their own pace. When they have started with the work, make it a point to check in with them regularly. If the person is new to the task, you can do periodical visits to ask how they're doing and monitor their progress. If the person is more experienced and has a better grasp on the task already, you can do away with fewer follow-ups and just ask for updates via email or through a monitoring system that's accessible to the both of you. Resist being too controlling or constantly looking over their shoulder to check on their every move. Focus more on the results, less on the procedures.

Once the work is finished, evaluate. Is the work fully complete and of good quality? Were the expectations met? Make your assessment and provide your feedback. Solicit for their input and open a discussion so you can both address challenges, if any, to improve how tasks were delegated within your team.

If outputs are unsatisfactory, discuss areas for improvement and ask for a rework. Allow them the additional time to learn to do the job properly. Don't accept a poorly done job. It robs the person the opportunity to acquire the skills from the task. Also, if you accept a substandard output, you will probably need to do it all over yourself. This invalidates the very reason why you delegated the task to another person, to begin with.

On the other hand, when good work is returned to you, acknowledge their efforts and give commendations when they have done an exceptional job. Make sure you recognize and reward their efforts. Lastly and most importantly, don't forget to thank them.

Here are some additional reminders to take note of when delegating tasks to your team:

Have the right people

The first thing is to ensure that you have the right people on your team. If you want to delegate effectively, you must have the people you can delegate too. You also need to have good knowledge of your team's skills, interests, motivations, and other traits. When selecting whom you're going to delegate an assignment, you need to know who's the most capable and most willing to do it well. Look beyond their work experiences. A person with only 5 years of experience that is obviously skilled and enthusiastic could be a better choice compared to someone who has twice as many years of experience but is not as capable.

Be engaging

Delegation involves a person-to-person approach, building effective and meaningful relationships with your people, especially those whom he works with toward the achievement of project objectives. Constantly engage your team and cultivate an atmosphere of respect, trust, and interdependence. This will lead to increased morale and motivation that will make them more understanding of the project objectives and more open to accepting additional tasks for the success of the project.

Be professional

Make sure you don't unknowingly fall into having a "favorite" person to assign tasks to or a "friend" among your team whom you want to go easy on and avoid entrusting complicated assignments to. Be mindful, professional, and fair with your team when delegating. Entrust tasks to people who deserve the opportunity and whom you know will deliver by choosing objectively and without bias.

Be clear

Be very clear about the tasks you are delegating. Set expectations comprehensively–specify what outputs are expected, how soon they should be done, who is involved, and the likes. Poorly defined tasks can result in poor results and failure to meet deadlines.

Be specific

When giving assignments, make sure you provide all the necessary information your team will need to get the job done right and on time. Some may even need an outline or an overview of instructions on how to get the job done right. Remember to be clear and specific to avoid uncertainty and miscommunication.

Be fair and realistic with timelines

It's understandable to want things done immediately with efficiency and precision. As a project leader, you are equipped with the technical skills to perform in such a way. However, your team members may require more time with their learning curve. You also must consider that they may have an existing workload that may be affected. Be considerate about the amount of work they already have. Don't push beyond a reasonable amount of work that they can handle. This can cause significant stress and affect their productivity and morale.

Give a time frame. You want your team to feel that you trust them enough to work on their own pace, especially considering that the task you are delegating to them are additional items on their plate. But providing a particular time frame will give them a sense of urgency to ensure that they complete it efficiently. When delegating, provide deadlines that are realistic. Giving too little time can put them under pressure and trigger them to lose motivation. Choosing a far-off deadline can also slow them down and promote procrastination.

Be empowering

Cultivate in your team a sense of ownership for the tasks delegated to them. Allow them the freedom to work how they wish but hold them accountable for the job. Require them to prepare and present regular progress reports. Make them understand that this is not just additional work for them, but this is an opportunity for them to prove themselves as efficient and responsible leaders. Giving them this much control over a higher assignment empowers them and uplifts them as professionals.

Be available

Delegating doesn't mean leaving your team all on their own. They should be able to come to you should they have questions or concerns about their tasks. Take care of the delegates. Ask how they are doing and if check if they encounter problems. If necessary, provide coaching to help them learn the ropes of the task. If they ask for your support, make sure you are there for them.

Be generous with authority

The need to delegate often arises because of time constraints at the end of the project leader. You may become overwhelmed with the amount of work needed to be done, so no longer able to provide hands-on guidance and specific instructions at all times. In cases like this, don't hesitate to appoint a person in the team to be your "lead" for a specific area or function. This person will be your go-to person to act as the officer-in-charge of that function in your place to ensure that the wheels are turning smoothly where everything is in place and everyone is able to work harmoniously. How you select that person can be tricky, however. If possible, appoint someone who has managerial or supervisory experience and has a good working relationship with everyone involved in the project. Don't look at this approach as an admission that you are not capable of handling your task as project manager. Delegating an extent of your authority to someone else allows the person opportunities for professional and leadership development. You're not only making your work easier; you're also molding future leaders within your team.

Be trusting

After giving out assignments, try to keep your hands off the work as much as possible. With your experience and competence, you have a strong grasp of how a certain job should be done. But delegating means allowing your people the space to be creative and innovative on their own means and trusting them to deliver the best results and project outcomes. Remember, your way is not necessarily the only or the best way. Avoid watching over their shoulders while they work. It can alienate your people and give them the feeling that you don't trust them. Also, it takes too much unnecessary effort and time on your end.

Let them come up with ideas and find their unique approach to the tasks at hand. Provide them with an avenue to give their inputs and recommendations on how to do things better. Keep in mind that as a project manager, your focus should be more on the results, less on the process. Let this be their opportunity to prove themselves and step up to the challenge. This will cultivate work relationships, built on trust and successes.

Be patient

Initially, you may observe that the person you have delegated a task to takes longer to complete the assignment. Keep in mind that because you are an expert in the field, you are used to a faster pace. The person you have delegated the task to, on the other hand, may still be learning. Be patient, the same way a teacher is patient with a student. If you have selected the right person for the task and you have delegated the task correctly, you will see that the person will adapt accordingly and improve in time.

Be enabling

Delegate to the lowest possible organizational level. The people who are hands-on are often those who have the most intimate familiarity with the details of the everyday work in the project life cycle. This knowledge and their direct exposure to the project makes them strong candidates to entrust tasks to. Enabling them can increase workplace efficiency while at the same time, develop them further as professionals.

Be encouraging

Support creative and innovative thinking from people you delegate tasks to. Even when they have visions on the matter that are different from yours, provide encouragement. Rather than countering their opinion, simply drop indirect suggestions for them to consider. Avoid "upward delegation." When the person encounters challenges in the task delegated to him, don't let them simply give up on the responsibility and revert it back to you. Engage them in constructive discussions, ask for their recommendations, encourage them to deliberate and decide, and then provide your support and counsel. Don't provide the solutions directly; encourage them to find solutions on their own so they will be empowered.

Be practical with your management style

As we discussed in chapter 3, management styles vary. There are leaders who are lenient in terms of supervision, whereas there are some who are more comfortable being constantly involved in all project activities. When you delegate, however, you want your team to feel that you trust them enough to keep enough distance while they attend to their tasks, while at the same time, being able to monitor the progress of their work. This is where a reporting system will come in handy. Set in place a non-disruptive centralized reporting system for your team where they can regularly post updates on their tasks. This will give you access to information on how the project is progressing without having to personally check on each team member. It's a practical way to manage your team as it saves their time and yours and prevents disruptions in the flow of your work schedules. Moreover, this will serve as your official documentation of delegated tasks.

Be organized

Having your own personal tracking system also helps you stay organized. When delegating tasks, it's unlikely you'll be delegating only to one person. Make sure you're noting down who's doing what. Keep your own log of the tasks you've delegated and the point person for each job. Monitor their progress from the reporting system and have your own records of status reports. This will help you stay in the loop of what's going on; analyze the pacing of the project cycle and check if any adjustments are needed.

Be responsive and prove feedback

Don't forget to acknowledge progress when tasks are delivered with efficiency and precision. Not only does providing positive feedback boost morale and motivation, but the team who works hard deserves it. It helps them stay focused, and it reinforces the objectives and goals of your project. Be their constant motivator by helping them focus on the returns if they are able to complete the tasks. Discuss how their success can result in financial rewards, future opportunities, and other desirable consequences. Motivated employees are more likely to be productive and enthusiastic about their work.

Again, at first glance delegating tasks may seem like too much of a hassle. Doing the job yourself is easier and faster, plus you'll be more confident and assured with the output. When done effectively, however, delegation has more advantages that outweigh the growing pains of mastering the skill:

- Effective delegation can significantly expand the amount of work that you and your team can deliver altogether. Having more people do more work leads to more successes.

- Effective delegation trains your people to take on higher responsibilities and function with minimal supervision.

- Effective delegation helps you maximize your time efficiently and focus on bigger tasks such as coming up with innovative ideas for project improvements, developing strategies and new processes, and strengthening connections with your stakeholders and other potential collaborators, all geared towards to achievement of project objectives.

Effective delegation empowers your team to be accountable for the project. You are teaching them more responsibility and motivating them to step up their game.

Yes, delegating tasks will appear like managing less because you become less hands-on with the task and more dependent on your people to get things done. Keep in mind, however, it's the manager who manages the least that leads the best.

CHAPTER 7 FIRING SOMEONE

"Maybe when we face a tragedy, someone, somewhere is preventing a bigger tragedy from happening."
— **Kamand Kojouri**

Many people would argue that one of the hardest things a manager must do to be successful is terminating employees when necessary.

The common idea is that termination is capital punishment in every organization. Being fired would be the worst thing to happen to anyone whether you're the employee or the employer. Not only does it put them in a difficult situation where they would need to confront an employee, but it also places them at risk of feeling guilty and anxious. You would be taking away a person's job, which is their source of income. This will affect not just the individual, but their families as well. You would think, how could you do that to someone, especially someone you have worked with and know personally? Then this also leads you to ask, how much are you helping that person and your organization by keeping them even if there are the telltale signs that they must be let go?

The bad behavior of a good employee can be corrected. This is ideally the route to take when you have a problematic employee in your team. It is a part of your job to keep everyone in check and help them identify and address areas of improvement in their individual performances throughout a given project. This includes exerting the effort to modify problematic behavior. After all, the person was hired or selected for the project because they showed promise. You, or someone saw the potential, competence, and character, which you believed was the right fit for your team. If they have proven themselves to be a valuable employee and team player at some point and you see them going through a bad phase in the middle of the project life cycle, it might be worth your time to implement corrective techniques that will help them get back on track. When there is an issue of poor performance, allow them time to improve. Conduct performance reviews so they would know how they are doing. As much as possible, be blunt about their performance and give them a surge of urgency to "up their game" by giving verbal warnings. When your gut instinct is to let someone go at the first sign of issues, you're missing the opportunity to modify problematic behavior and save an otherwise good person in your team. Additionally, you can spare yourself from the cost and burden of turnover. But if the person still doesn't improve after giving them grace periods, don't wait further to make your decision.

There is no better way to illustrate this fact that with the story of Ryan Turner:

Ryan Turner's cigarette was burning down to its butt at an alarming rate; such was the intensity of each of his tokes. The allotted 'smoking zone' was a pint-sized little area at the back of the staff car park—a grimy corner between an unused garage and the back of the (now defunct) men's loos. Ryan looked at home here; his eyes were sleepy, hair uncombed and tweed jacket badly scuffed on one side. He liked being out here though, alone, with only his anxieties and his cigarette for company, a solid hundred meters away from his office and the increasing mess his latest project was turning into.

Ryan worked for an ad agency and was head of scripting on an exciting project the company had landed. The day had begun with his morning meeting, a daily ritual Ryan had put in place to make sure his team was on track. Over the past couple of weeks, it had turned into an opportunity to remind Ryan that his team certainly wasn't on track. They'd derailed early in the project and were now on a different set of tracks altogether, final destination: clear your desk and find the nearest job center.

Before his cigarette could burn its last light, Ryan pulled another from his pack and set it alight—a delaying tactic as much as anything else could. In that morning's meeting, he had told one of his scriptwriters, Sasha that he wanted to talk to him in his office at 10AM. Sasha had been one of the main reasons the project was heading straight into the abyss and Ryan's inbox had been bombarded with emails from the rest of his team, each berating and lambasting Sasha's contribution. They all wanted him out and Ryan knew he had to go. It was now 9:56 and Ryan was wishing he could hide in this grimy little corner for the rest of the day. Conflict was something he tried to avoid at all costs and the thought of giving Sasha the boot was the reason his pack of anxiety-taming cigarettes was now empty.

As he filled his lungs with another hefty cloud of smoke Ryan spotted the beaming figure of Fred Sanchez gliding swiftly in his direction. Fred was the studio manager at the agency and his team was currently working on the design and resource side of the new project.
"Hey Turner, thought you said you were quitting that stuff?" Fred said as he pulled out his shiny new e-cig.
"It's a work in progress," Ryan said sheepishly. He was lying, of course, knowing six others had preceded the cigarette currently between his fingers that morning.
"You know, I used to be a twenty-a-day man." Ryan was aware of this.
"My wife told me she was pregnant, threw a full packet straight in the bin the moment I found out."
"What, just like that?"
"Just like that. Bought myself this bad boy instead," Fred said as he blew out the type of cloud, you'd expect to see come from a steam engine. "Thing is you can't half-ass it with the things that matter, you've got to be straight, direct. Just do what's got to be done."
Ryan envied his efficiency.
"How are things your side anyway? Script coming along nicely I hope?"
"Getting there Fred, couple hiccups but nothing out the ordinary," he said, lying again of course. "Absolutely, got a few bumps on our side of the road as well but we'll be dandy soon enough," Fred replied with a confident grin.
Ryan checked his watch: 10:01 AM. "Shoot! I got to run. I'll see you soon."
"You better have one of these," raising his e-cig in the air, "next time I catch you out here! Do what's got to be done!"

It was now 10:09 AM and Ryan sat in his office still awaiting the arrival of Sasha. He could see through a crack in his blinds that his ill-disciplined scriptwriter was nattering away on his phone by the coffee machine. Ryan opened his door and beckoned Sasha into his office. Sasha gestured two minutes with his fingers, Ryan reluctantly shook his head and returned to his desk.
"Heyyy my man Ryan, how are ya' buddy?" Sasha cheerfully said as he

bowled through the door about ten minutes later.

"Take a seat." Ryan tried to say in as serious a tone as he could muster. "Wooow, somebody's in a bad mood!"

"We need to talk about this project Sasha. I've been getting a lot of grief from the rest of the team about you."

"About me?!" Sasha sounded genuinely shocked, "Damn snakes!"

"It's not just them, I've been watching you. And quite frankly you've been taking the mick." There was no reply from Sasha.

"Yesterday you turned up to the writer's room with a script that was three drafts old. And on Monday, you were supposed to go with Karen to audition those actors. She had to cancel on them after waiting an hour for you at the train station." Ryan steadied himself. "Sasha I'm sorry but you're off…"

Sasha quickly butted in. "Listen, man, me and you go way back, like, little league way back. We went to prom in the same damn limo man! You might be my manager but you're my friend first. Okay, maybe I've been a teeny bit off the ball lately, but I've had stuff going on man. I'll sort it out. I promise." He was really tugging the heartstrings. "Just give me a second chance."

"This is about your fifth chance." Ryan looked down and sighed. "Just take the afternoon off and sort yourself out. Come back here tomorrow ready to go. Last chance."

The big smile returned to Sasha's face. "You're a legend bud. Works well for me. I've got a parcel coming this afternoon, just been on the phone to the guys before I came in here actually. Got myself the new Xbo…"

"Sasha please!!"

"You'll see a new me tomorrow morning," Sasha said swinging open the office door, "those damn snakes can't bring us down brother!"

Three days had passed, and Ryan was sat around a table in the conference room with all the other project leads. Amongst them was Fred Sanchez, currently updating the rest of the table on his team's progress.

"We've found a great spot for the shoot. Took a little bit longer than I'd hoped but after cutting some slack, so to speak, I've got it all set up." There was a proud look on his face. Ryan was next to hold the floor and he stumbled a little before finally spitting out his words. "The script still needs work." There was an awkward silence.

"How much work?" Trevor Ryley, the company founder sternly asked. "Probably about a week. Give or take."

"Ryan, you said the same thing last week. We're two weeks out now; they're expecting me to send them a shooting script tomorrow. What's been going on?"

Ryan hesitated for a moment; he didn't want to tell them what was really going on. He couldn't tell his contemporaries that he'd been too much of a coward to boot his old friend off the project; the old friend who'd spent the last three days throwing the script even farther off course by causing a huge riff in the writer's room by sending out a group email detailing the exact nature of his peer's 'snaky' behavior. No, he couldn't tell them that.

"We've had a few differences in 'artistic' opinion," he said, "I'll have a shooting script over to you by Friday. Promise," he immediately regretted saying, knowing very well this was a promise he couldn't keep.

"Okay. Don't make me do something I don't want to do Ryan," Trevor said, rounding up the meeting.

Ryan stood in the smoking area contemplating his fate, 'What will kill me first?' He wondered, 'Trevor Ryley or these damn cancer sticks?' A flash of light suddenly caught his eye. It was the sun beaming brightly off Fred's walkie-talkie looking e-cigarette.

"Still a work in progress then ay' Turner?"

"We'll have a script by Friday, Fred."

"I was talking about those," Fred said signaling towards Ryan's cigarette.

"Oh. Yeah. I'm cutting down." Lying again.

"What did I tell you? You've got to go all out. Just do what's got to be done. No messing around." He chugged his vape. "Remember those bumps in the road I was telling you about the other day? I bulldozed those right out. Found out two of my team were messing about on the job, they nearly lost me the location. Had to do my hardest to get it back."

"What did you do?"

"Kicked 'em straight off the team. They'll be making coffees and hovering floors for the next week. No messing about."

Ryan quickly stubbed out his cigarette and made a dart back to the office. "I'll catch up with you later Fred. Something I've got to do," he said from a distance.

Ryan walked up to Sasha's desk with a meaningful conviction. It was vacant. He turned to see him on his phone by the water dispenser. Ryan stormed over.

"Sasha, my office. Now."

"Two secs buddy, I'm just…"

"Now!" Ryan wasn't messing around.

The pair sat either side of an unorganized desk. Sasha tried to lighten the mood by telling his old friend some Xbox-related story, but Ryan quickly shut him down. "I don't know what you thought you were doing with that email nonsense. Eve and Bill nearly walked when they read it. They thought I was on your side!"

"Let them walk. I've always said they're second-rate writers."

Ryan sighed. "I'm going to need you to sit this one out Sasha. We'll find you something else, maybe something smaller, less of a team project."

"You're firing me?!"

"Think of it as a time-out. I'm going to be the one clearing my desk if this script isn't ready by Friday." Sasha shook his head and laughed, saying: "The only reason you'll be clearing your desk on Friday is to make room for the gigantic bonus they'll be giving you. As I tried to tell you earlier before you rudely cut me off, I made some pretty tasty progress on the script last night. I met a guy, on Xbox Live of all places, who happens to work in the industry. Cut a long story short, we talked for like three hours about the project, I told him everything. He gave me a massive list of ideas, lines, jokes. It's killer stuff. I've been drafting them all in an email this morning." Ryan immediately perked up. "When can you send me this email?"

"It will be with you within the hour," Sasha smugly said. "You know I've always got your back buddy."

It was Friday lunchtime and Fred Sanchez had popped to the smoking area before that day's project manager meeting. They were all to assemble in the conference room to discuss the well- overdue shooting script. As he blew another thick cloud, a quizzical look appeared on Fred's face. Where was his friend Ryan Turner? The look on his face quickly turned into a smile. He'd kicked the habit, he thought. Did what needed to be done. Didn't even need to downgrade to an e-cig, a clean break! The moment was cut short as a curly-haired figured emerged with a lit cigarette in his mouth. It was Sasha. "Hey, Sasha! Long time no see. I'm just about to go and read the script you guys have put together for us."

Sasha shook his head. "Good luck with that."

"What?" the quizzical look had returned.

"There is no script. Haven't you heard? They pulled the plug on the project. They were approached by a different agency, pitched them some amazing idea, they had a script put together and everything. Killer stuff apparently." Sasha took another drag.

"You must be joking."

"It gets worse. They just fired Ryan. Said that if he'd got a draft together when they asked none of this would have happened. Bastards man! I'd do anything for that guy, he's like my brother."

Poor performance is not the only reason to make cuts in your team and organization. Perhaps you have that person who has a serious attitude problem or who enjoys bullying other people in your team. In your company's code of conduct, you will find specific grounds for termination that may be either disciplinary or performance-based in nature that cannot be resolved. Let's discuss some major red flags that will tell you when that person needs to be let go:

- The person has been caught to have repeatedly lied or provided false information with the purpose to deceive. It's easy to say that white lies are harmless, but lies, no matter how small, are lies. Dishonesty can greatly reflect a person's credibility and professionalism. There are different ways in which a person can be professionally dishonest. One is through lying by intentionally providing false statements. Another is through lies of omission where that person purposefully leaves out important pieces of business-related information. A third way is through obfuscation, which is the act of modifying statements to make a piece of information unclear or inaccurate. A person whose integrity you can't be certain of has no place in your team. Because your project relies on the interdependence among your team, you must know that you can trust your people. When you can no longer trust a team member, you will have to let that person go in one way or another.

- When a person can't do the job. This is a point where we emphasize the importance of carefully selecting the right people to get in your team. There may be instances where you had no voice in the selection process and you have someone who does not naturally have the skills necessary to perform the fundamental requirements of the job. You can exert efforts to have that person trained, coached, practiced, and mentored. You can even give extensions for their learning curve. However, if that person still fails to function and deliver the desired outcomes, you and your team may be wasting time and resources in training one poorly performing person. There's also probably somebody else who is doing extra work to cover up that person's shortcoming. Basically, their lack of ability is compromising the collective performance and output of the team. If you can relate to all these, it might be time to fire that person from the project or from the organization. Remember, you are working towards common goals for the success of the project, not just toward the success of one person.

- The person doesn't fit in and is upsetting the team's morale and performance. We noted in Chapter 2 that there is strength in diversity. Having a group of diverse individuals encourages creative thinking and complementary teamwork. The issue, however, is if there that person who purposely resists blending in with the existing culture of the team and refuses to accept the team's set of shared values that binds them together. Perhaps that person has the personality of an office bully–taking pleasure in pushing people around and their arrogance undermines everyone they work with. They are indifferent to the feelings of their teammates and they don't care as much about the project or your stakeholders. Basically, people are happier when they are not around. No matter how hard you try; you can't turn around their attitude. In cases like this, you must be very careful not to make discriminating judgments. Be remarkably objective when using misfit as a reason to have someone removed from your team. State evidence-based information, which will prove that that person's resistance to embracing the team's existing culture is damaging collective morale and performance.

- The person can't keep commitments and deliver. Whether it's her promise to be punctual at work or to complete an assignment before the due date, that person just can't seem to deliver as she promises. Because everyone has unique roles to play in the team, her failure to keep her commitments affects almost everyone else. Other workers may be depending on her to cover a shift, or her output may be a prerequisite to complete a bigger assignment. It's one thing when someone occasionally misses a deadline, but it's another thing when that person not only fails to deliver on time, but she also fails to inform you and give you a "heads up" about it. When that person neglects her commitments and her responsibility to inform you about any challenges related to her work, you might need to terminate her.

- The person has no regard for a company's code of conduct. Upon hiring, employers should make sure to present their company's policies including the code of conduct and discipline. It's their responsibility to ensure that employees accept and adhere to these policies as guidelines for ethical behavior in the workplace. Any employee who has proven to violate these policies and engage in unethical workplace behavior despite being given ample time to correct their behavior must be dealt with accordingly–no exceptions. Say, for example, that person has had issues with attendance for some time now. She is frequently late for work and her tardiness has been affecting the rest of the team's performance. You have initially begun by calling her out and giving warnings in accordance with the company's progressive discipline policy (for example, first verbal warning, first written warning, a second written warning with suspension). She gives her assurance that she will do better and come on time—which she does for the first several days. Until she starts missing the clock again. This is where you draw the line. No one should be excused from the policies. This is included in the terms of employment and employees need to be accountable for their actions. If they are unable to abide by the rules and regulations and exhibit no regard for the company policies that person must be let go. Remember, rules are rules, not suggestions.

As the project manager and the leader of your project team, you want to strike the right balance between looking out for your people and ensuring the success of your project. However, you must keep in mind to put the company's interest first. For some time, you probably have exerted efforts to correct their behavior or improve poor performance but to no avail. When you arrive at the end of this, you have carefully planned out the steps to do the least amount damage to the organization and to the rest of your team. In carrying out terminations, it's critical that the process is done properly, respectfully, and professionally.

Losing one person in a project team is a major change in your project. As discussed in Chapter 4, most of the changes you will encounter are unforeseen. Of course, you didn't hire the person with the thought of eventually letting them go in the middle of the project. However, due to certain circumstances, this is a decision that had to be made and an action that must be done. Firing someone means losing a player in your team. This means everybody else may be affected and will have to make adjustments to keep the wheels continuously running. Similar to any change in the project plan, you will have to carefully plan this. In this specific situation, it's important that you develop a well-thought and comprehensive transition plan before you let someone go so you and your team will not be left scrambling when you have made the decision that the person must be let go. Transition Plan templates are available at: www.wranglingsquirrels.com/resources

The decision is final, irrevocable, and non-negotiable. Firing someone may not ever become comfortable to do. But with these steps in mind, you may be able to get through it with the least pain and discomfort for both of you. **Create a plan**

Begin with how you will be informing the employee. Schedule a one-on-

one meeting with the person involved at a carefully selected day and time. According to experts, doing it early in the week encourages the employee to move forward in making their own transition plan to find another job. It also reduces the chance that he will spend the weekend wallowing about it.

Develop a succession plan. If you are already seeing that the person's track is towards termination, it will be helpful to start considering potential candidates who can take over their jobs when they are to let go. Don't neglect to inform your stakeholders about the staffing changes as well. Prepare a continuity plan for the work that person will be leaving behind. Check his workload and assess how his absence will affect the work of the rest of the team and your project timelines. Plan how you can divide the work and reassign tasks among the rest of the team while you don't have an identified replacement yet.

Prepare the paperwork

It's imperative that the termination process be well-documented. If the person is being let go for poor performance, compile his performance reviews. If the employee has committed a serious policy violation, prepare a copy of the code of discipline and the incident report. Have everything in writing and make sure that these were accordingly presented to the employee prior to the termination, so as not to catch them off guard. These documents will also help you defend your actions legally if necessary.

Consult and seek for counsel

To fire someone is a major decision to make. You want to ensure that you are making a sound, objective, and solid decision when terminating an employee. Don't go through this undertaking alone. Consult with your senior manager and the HR Department about this decision. The HR Department will be your biggest ally as they have a sufficient grasp in terms of technicalities and legal implications.

When deliberating your decision, try to imagine yourself defending your decision to a counsel. Deliberate on all aspects of your decision and look for anything that can be wrongly used to suggest that the person is being fired for reasons other than their individual performance. Specifically, identify the primary reasons for the termination by providing data and explaining the previous course of actions implemented to correct the behavior. Prepare your Incident Log to provide it as the official document of reference (to be discussed in further detail later in this chapter). Think of all possible disputes against your decision, including personal attacks and subjective rebukes.

Write a script

To tell someone that they are fired, either from a function, project or job, is hardly a walk in the park. For most people, it's awkward, uncomfortable, and sometimes nerve-wracking. If you will be delivering the news yourself and you are not the confrontational type of person, it will be helpful to prepare a script where all the important facts are listed down with the important details. This way, you are less likely to forget critical information when you break the news. You will be able to explain the reasons for the decision. If you can, stick to your script. Remember, when you meet the person, the objective is to inform then about a final and irrevocable decision. Don't make the conversation longer than necessary. Focus on specific behavior, state the fact and the actions, and then close. It isn't necessary to explain the decision if you have previously given coaching and feedback on their performance. The aim is not to counsel the person, not to apologize for the circumstance, and not to give them the opportunity to negotiate.

Be straightforward. Get straight to the point. "Hi, James. Please have a seat. I'm afraid I have some bad news for you."

Use concise statements. Speak in the past tense. "Your performance has been a concern of ours in the past 3 months. We have previously discussed your inability to meet your KPIs. Last month's report showed that despite efforts to support you and provide opportunities to improve your performance, you were still unable to meet the desired numbers. The management team and I have decided that we must let you go. Effective today, your employment has been terminated." The employee may have questions and even negative reactions. Let them know that the decision is final, and the termination has already taken effect.

Pay attention to how the employee responds

Although you can expect some predictable reactions from them such as the shock, denial, grief, perhaps even anger, pay close attention to how the employee responds. Be sensitive to non-verbal cues. Knowing how the employee is taking the news will help you phrase your next statements. Have a box of tissues ready on your desk—just in case that person may become emotional. When the employee has an aggressive personality and there is a chance that he may retaliate during the conversation, consider having a witness from HR, or another manager present in the meeting. In very rare cases, you might also look at having security on standby should the employee become violent and physical. This is not to intimidate the employee but to ensure the safety and security of everyone else in the office.

Be specific about what happens next

Make sure to cover everything important such as his final pay, benefits, unused vacation leave, references, ongoing assignments, and transition of responsibilities. Be sure to answer every question he might have and avoid leaving any items open. This can give the employee false hopes and he might consider this as an opportunity to negotiate this status. Tell the employee that HR will be reaching out to him for further instructions and information.

Wrap it up with swiftly

Close the meeting by thanking the individual. "We do appreciate your contributions to the team and to the project. Thank you for efforts for the past three months you have spent with us." Walk with the employee toward his desk and wait as he picks up his personal items. Collect any company assets that he might have, such as office keys, mobile phone, laptop, and the likes. Allow him a few minutes to say a quick goodbye to the rest of the team and walk with him to the exit. If their response has been reasonable, offer your hand to shake his, wish him well, and say your farewell.

Evaluate the impact

That door closing does not signify the end of this process. Ask to sit down with other managers and key persons whom that person may have worked with to conduct an assessment and identify possible learning opportunuties that can help you and the organization spot potential performance and attitude issues ahead of time.

Make sure you also cover all loose ends. Terminate their access to information systems such as email, intranet, and the like. If they open transactions with external partners, send out communications that the person is no longer connected with your team and the organization and provide an alternative contact.

Remember that your attitude will ultimately determine the course of the conversation. Be mindful with your statements so as not to trigger any unwanted emotions or retaliation from the employee. Here are some statements to avoid:

I understand how you feel.

If you have never experienced being fired, don't ever say this because, well, it's not true at all. If you have been terminated at one point in your life, it might not be in the exact same circumstance. The person also might be going through other situations in his personal life, which you know nothing of. This may be difficult now but eventually; you will understand that this could be a blessing in disguise and may be the best that could have happened. It is bad thing for him at the moment and will be a bad thing for him as he transitions from having a job one minute and being laid off the next.

You should have known this would happen.

Even when he probably has anticipated this, avoid using this to justify the decision. Stick with the facts and the reasons for the termination.

Speak with your team

After the ex-employee and has left the premises, talking to the colleagues who worked alongside that position is a good idea. Keep it simple, do not reveal reasons for the decision, that is confidential information. Simply let them know the person is no longer with the team and explain to them how it will affect the team moving forward. Until the position is filled, responsibilities may need to be delegated. Ensure everyone knows what to do.

It's natural if you will feel compassion toward an employee you're letting go of. After all, this person we're talking about one has a family to go home to and needs to provide for, also one whom you have worked and spent time with. However, don't forget about the rest of your team who do manage to do their jobs well and deliver unwavering results. If one of them has been under-performing for a significant period, they may have been putting in extra work to make up for his incompetence.

Here are additional tips that can help you get through the process peacefully:

Be self-aware. When making the decision to fire someone, keep in mind that your own attitude towards the person you need to fire can determine your next steps in the termination process. Take time to do some introspection and be aware of your own ideas, feelings, and thoughts toward the person. This will help you stay objective and unbiased in the decision-making process. Before arriving at a final verdict, review previous corrective actions that had been done in an effort to salvage that person's position, and make sure the decision is justified.

Having that talk is never easy. But the same way that you rip off a band-aid quickly to feel as less pain as possible when you fire someone, try to take as little time as possible. Schedule it at the soonest time available. Dragging out the bad news won't hurt any less when you deliver it. There's no point in prolonging the process because the decision has already been made and cannot be amended.

Quick tips to remember:
- Be precisely clear with your intentions. Don't beat around the bush with small talk because this can send ambiguous messages and the employee will be confused by mixed signals. You need to be very clear to your employees. In the same way they fully understand when they are hired, they should also understand when they are fired.

- Avoid apologizing for the decision. That person has put it on himself or herself. Apologizing just helps them shift the blame to you in their mind. They are responsible for their fate and they should take accountability for the consequences.

- Do not provide opportunities for negotiations. It would be unbecoming to have the person ask or even beg to keep their job. Tell them that you will provide the support necessary to walk them through the process, but the decision has been made.

- Turn off your own emotions. Stay composed throughout the entire process. Remove compassion from the conversation. Simply stick with the facts and state the reasons. Adding emotions to the picture will send a wrong message and may complicate the process and trigger an emotional situation. Tell them you wish them well but say no more.

- Treat the person with the utmost respect at all times, even after they are let go. Give them the opportunity to leave with their pride and dignity intact. Don't humiliate them. When you break the news about their termination, make sure you do it behind closed doors. Keep in mind that employees talk, and word goes around fast. You want to ensure that the final interaction that a person has with your organization is one with a positive note and will not spark any unwanted controversy from that person.

- Make sure all the actions you take in the termination process are legal. Double-check the employee's contract and other relevant documents. If his contract and your company policies state that he cannot be terminated on the grounds you have against him, don't proceed immediately. Consult with your company lawyer. The last thing you want is a lawsuit against you for unlawful termination.

- Don't prolong the process once the decision to terminate has been made. The faster you pull the plug, the faster you and your team can execute the transition plan and make up for the shortcomings of the persons to bring the project life cycle at its maximum level of operation. If an individual has proven himself to be invaluable in the project despite attempts to coach, train, and develop him, don't hold on to the hope that things may still work out.

- Letting a non-performing individual in your project team go may feel like a sigh of relief at first. Although there are adjustments that you need to make, you'd think that losing the person also means solving the problem they left behind and moving forward to implementing solutions. However, a realization may hit you: someone you know and had worked with just lost a job. He will be going home to his family and will be telling that he'd been fired. He will be temporarily incapable to support them. You think the termination did not just affect him–it affected his entire family. Now, this can leave you with a feeling of intense guilt. You may even start to question your decision. In moments like this, you must remind yourself that there is a reason that the person has been terminated. Keep in mind that when you let go of a person who is slowing you, your team, and your project, it's not because you want to make his life miserable, it's because he is making yours and your team's miserable.

- The separation doesn't end after getting rid of the problem employee. When a player on your team leaves his place, you'll have to immediately check on his work and make sure that the operations of the project won't be disrupted by his absence. In case you've let go of an underperforming employee, you might have to dig through their work files to look over any tasks that have yet to complete or are in need of re-work. This must be done quickly before any loose ends compromise your team's collective performance and upset your stakeholders.

- You'll also have to face the reality of finding a new person to fill their place. Do take note that it's costlier to hire someone new than must retain a current employee. You will have to go through the entire hiring process, which will take much of your time and use up your resources. But this doesn't mean that, for the sake of convenience, it's better to keep an under-performer or an errant worker in your team. Remember to think long term. Will the price of letting go of someone whose performance (or lack of it) can create a serious dent in your project be worth more than the price of hiring someone new?

- When you fire someone, you can't avoid having people talk about it. There will be questions and concerns: What did he do? Why are we letting people go? Who could be next? Are we in danger? Be prepared for this. As much as possible, be transparent with your team by providing as much non-confidential information to help them understand the situation. Exhibit a positive mindset and assure them that you will be leading them in moving forward to providing better services for the achievement of your project goals. Remember that your attitude toward the situation will greatly impact how your team will perceive this circumstance and affect the overall culture.

When termination is fairly made, justified, and carried out professionally, you and your team will reap the benefits of losing a team member. Frustrations from having to deal with difficulties brought about by the individual will subside and the rest of the team will realize that you have a good team and a good work environment.

When you refuse to accept that the under-performers need to be let go and allow them to continue in their positions comfortably and without the fear of losing their post, you're basically telling the good, talented, and performing employees that this is acceptable behavior and that you're willing to settle for substandard performance in your team. This can greatly affect the morale and motivation of your team members. Eventually, they will feel frustrated and may even pack up and leave in the search for other jobs. Those who will choose to stay will be those who are okay with a manager who has low standards for performance and works ethics. The absence of efforts from the manager to correct bad behavior is taken by his staff as a message of approval.

Remember: In any work setting, you must give the highest regard to professionalism. Being professional means being fair and just. If the non-performers are tolerated while those who do deliver are expected to continue to do their jobs well, you can cause serious strife in your team. Bad employees can diminish the morale of the entire team and can affect their productivity. When you let go of under-performers, you give your good team players more space to move and excel in their work. You free them from the burden of having to carry a slacker in your team. You alleviate from the having to make up for the shortcomings of a slouch. You motivate them by showing that your team has no place for mediocrity and substandard performance.

While being compassionate tells us to give considerations, inadequate performance should not be tolerated in your project. You are the project team first and family second. You are a project manager first, and a friend second (or not at all). Remember, the reason why you should fire someone is to ensure that the rest of the team can work better, and the project can be assured of its success. The members of your project team are humans. Each one has their own personal feelings towards the person who had been fired. They will also have their own opinions about the decision to let go of the person and about you as the manager who handled the entire situation. Take note the way you manage every situation will ultimately influence how your team will perceive you as their leader, affecting the amount of control you have in managing them along the project life cycle.

Be transparent with your team. Leaving them confused and wondering can affect morale and upset their performance. It can also lead to increased levels of anxiety and stress among your team members.

Set a meeting with them and brief them accordingly. Present your continuity plan and assure them that you will be moving forward together. By applying what we've learned in Chapter 6, delegate some tasks and give out assignments while you haven't identified a replacement yet. Be clear about the priorities, appoint officers in charge, and put forward the over-all plan. Take the opportunity to revisit your company's values and policies. If there's one thing you can get from terminating someone, it's the timely chance to remind your people about acceptable and unacceptable behaviors and attitudes in the workplace. Be positive and encouraging. Remind them of your project objectives and collective goals. Bring their focus back to your common vision—which is the success of the project. The sooner you shake them out of their anxieties, the sooner you can get back on track and return your focus on the more important matter at hand—the project.

Keeping your team in the dark about a major change in your project such as losing a team member will lead into suspicion and uncertainties. If someone has been fired without any explanation or notice, you're leaving your team to speculate. To keep a harmonious relationship with your team, you to work in keeping their trust.

Making the decision to let someone go and executing the termination is a serious responsibility. It's difficult, but it's necessary, especially when that person is a serious threat to your team and to your project's success. When it's time to fire someone, make it as quick and as painless as possible, so long as you make it happen.

CHAPTER 8 CONFLICT MANAGEMENT

"Conflict, when handled correctly, strengthens." -Benjamin Watson

So far, we've identified the non-negotiable responsibilities of a project manager that you won't always find in your job description or in an academic course plan. We've talked about managing your own manager, dealing with sudden changes, doing negotiations and more. Now, we'll talk about another inevitable element in the life of a project manager: conflict.

Just like change, conflict is inevitable. Because you work with a number of unique individuals coming from different backgrounds that have diverse personalities, attitudes, values, needs, expectations, perspectives, resources, and so on, the potential for conflict is inescapable and often high.

Conflict can arise at any level in an organization and at any point in the project cycle. Some common causes of conflict are issues in resourcing, arguments about procedures, methodologies, materials, disputes in costs and expenditures, differences of opinions, disagreements on responsibilities, the delegation of tasks and scheduling, misaligned goals and objectives, and lastly but probably the most common is personality clashes.

Now, one would think conflict is a bad thing. Some would imagine brawls and battles when talking about conflict. However, in the workplace, conflict can be constructive, healthy, and beneficial in an organization. The trick is to make sure you, as project manager, are equipped with the sufficient skills to lead your team in recognizing, understanding, and resolving conflict through a professional and healthy approach.

There are typically two major kinds of conflict: constructive conflict, and destructive conflict. Conflict can reveal underlying issues concerning your project and within your team. This gives you the opportunity to confront these matters, identify problem areas, and determine the best solutions. Dealing with conflicts help to strengthen communication within your team's interests, goals, and other project concerns around these issues.

Being faced with conflict also teaches you and your team how to manage disagreements and disputes. Therefore, when future conflict arises, you would know which approaches are inappropriate and incongruous with your values as a project team. Constructive conflict provides your team members an avenue to grow and develop professionally and personally. In constructive conflict, individuals involved learn positively from the experience, teams become stronger, and disputes are resolved accordingly.

If a conflict is not managed the right way, it's detrimental to your team and to your project. A conflict becomes deconstructive when problems are ignored, issues are left undiscussed, and no solution has been identified. Basically, the problem is left to fester and it slowly, sometimes, invisibly, poisons the team's morale. It threatens individual well-being, work relationships, team unity, business partnerships, and other interpersonal relations, thus compromising project operations, harming business performance and results, and affecting your project's success.

Now, if you want to manage conflict, start by understanding what exactly it is and what are the elements that come into play when disagreements and disputes arise with the people involved. Conflict often involves several dynamics:

Perception of the goal: Individuals have different personalities and you might have people in your team who are highly competitive. This is not necessarily a bad thing. Competitive people are usually motivated, hardworking, disciplined, and results-driven. You want to have team players who are highly driven toward the success of the project. However, this can become a problem when their eyes are on the goal, but they also need to prove that they are better than the other people in your team, hence creating a sense of competition among your team members.

Perception of others: In this situation, competitiveness is heightened by an attitude of "me versus them." The aim is now to outshine the others, not to win as a team, perhaps not even to achieve the goals of the project. This can cause a divide within your team and squash team cohesiveness altogether.

View of other's actions: When the sense of competition among team members becomes profound, people become suspicious of other's behaviors. Rather than being cooperative, they are indifferent or, worse, combative toward each other and develop distorted perceptions of the behavior of others.

Definition of the problem: Sometimes, the smallest concerns can be blown out of proportion when it's not dealt with. It can accelerate problems, issues can be misconstrued, and the underlying issue can be lost in translation. This makes the situation more complicated and more challenging to manage.

Communication: A problematic work environment fosters mistrust and suspicion. This hinders your team from communicating in an open and honest manner, compromising the accuracy of information relevant to your project.

Group dynamics: Having a team where people do not fully trust each other and are competing against one another makes it difficult, if not impossible, to create a safe and open environment where they can work harmoniously and interdependently. As a result, you will have a team culture that defeats the purpose of working as a team.

The workplace culture, the personalities of the people in your team, and the interpersonal dynamics of work relationships are all factors that can contribute to the chances of conflict occurring in your project environment. In a nutshell, there are two major elements that strongly influences conflict: communication and emotion.

Try to recall conflicts you have encountered in the past. Often, disagreements and disputes are caused by a lack of information, misinformation, or no information at all. These could all have been prevented if there was a clear, accurate, and concise exchange of information through open and effective communication. Emotions can also contribute to rifts in the workplace. When feelings are enforced instead of business goals, you can expect a lot of trouble. As the project manager, you play a crucial role in influencing the environment whether intentionally or unintentionally. Being the leader of a team puts you in a position where even the seemingly trivial matters, such as arriving late for meetings or delaying approvals for requests, can cause small problems to fester and grow into bigger conflicts. As a project manager, you're constantly monitoring everyone's progress, looking at what's been done and what hasn't been done, checking their performance and picking through errors and mistakes. You are also responsible for chasing down decisions and answers, seeking out the people accountable and calling out the people responsible for any breach in the project plan. Without the right conflict resolution skills, your project and your team will suffer.

This can all sound overwhelming, especially when you're fairly new to this function. Note, however, that nobody is expecting you to be a superhero. In reality, you will not have all the capabilities to resolve every conflict you or your team will encounter.

What's crucial in conflict management is to cultivate an environment for your team where they feel comfortable to have open and direct communications with each other. It's also important to imbibe a culture of professionalism and idealism for them to seek the best possible solutions for the benefit of everyone and for the success of the project.

As previously mentioned, conflict, similar to change, is inevitable in projects. Being the leader of the project, one thing you should always be on your toes for are potential areas and situations where conflicts may arise. This will help you spot the conflict early and control the situation before the conflict manifests into something bigger.

When conflict is already present, be mindful to address it immediately. It's easy to put it off for another time and attend to seemingly more urgent and matters first. However, conflicts are like a ticking time bomb. If mismanaged or neglected, they can get worse over time and blow out of proportion, giving you an even bigger mess to take care of. This can have a severe impact on your people, your project, and even yourself.

Very rarely does conflict resolve itself so it's imperative you, as project leader, are proactive in managing them. There are five popular approaches to conflict management: Confronting, Compromising, Smoothing, Forcing, and Avoiding.

Our personalities often determine our initial and natural reaction and response to trying situations such as disagreeing with others or mediating a dispute between two other individuals. However, because of the diverse work dynamics of your project, conflict will arise. It will help you be well-versed with a handful of strategies and approaches you can use when managing conflict.

Confronting: Also known as problem-solving, integrating, collaborating, or win-win style, collaborating often entails involving the conflicting parties in a dialogue where they can discuss their concerns and put their heads together to arrive at a solution favorable to all of them. It attempts to incorporate different perspectives and insights to arrive at one solution that is agreed upon by everyone involved. This is an approach where the conflict is dealt with upfront and the end goal is to solve the problem head-on.

Confronting requires a cooperative attitude and open direct communication to solve the existing problem. It often takes a natural course when the conflict is relaxed and passive, and the needs of the opposing parties are not overly weighted or delicate. The confronting approach is ideal because bringing together the opposing parties to come up with mutually agreeable solutions poses little chance of the conflict escalating or leading to other problems. It can strengthen your status as project leader because you have a happier and more collaborative team. This approach takes effort, time, and a good set of interpersonal skills because confronting means laying everything out on the table and having people talk directly to each other about the issues even when it's uncomfortable.

One sample situation where a confronting approach applies to resolve conflict is when your team is having issues about schedules and coverage. Your team is made of diverse personalities who have different personal affairs outside the workplace. However, your project requires your team to be available in the workplace for coverage of the operations. Without a formal discussion about the schedule, your team is now unable to agree on who will be reporting at which period. Right away, you schedule a team meeting at the soonest possible time and have everyone attend and provide their inputs and recommendations on how to arrange the team's schedule.

There may be those who express that going on a graveyard shift will be too demanding for them, while some shared that due to household situations, they will be unable to come to cover afternoon shifts. Each person is given the opportunity to share their thoughts about the problem and what arrangement they would be most comfortable with. After exchanging viewpoints, you and the team have decided to set a rotating shift schedule for everyone to distribute the workload fairly while still allowing everyone the time to arrange for the change in schedules.

Confronting is best used in situations where:

The need for both parties must be met.
You want to save on cost (in terms of mediation, to be discussed further later).
You have enough time for both parties to meet and discuss personally.
The parties involved have a sense of trust between each other.
Both parties are willing to identify their strengths and find a way to work together.

Compromising: Often referred to as the reconcile or "give and take" style. Compromising means to bargain in order to arrive at a mutually favorable solution. Similar to confronting, when compromising the solution, you will look for one where everyone walks away satisfied to a certain degree with little effort exerted. The main difference is, when you compromise, one or both parties will have to give in on the other's ideas and suggestions to resolve the conflict. This may mean that adjustments will have to be made to meet both of their needs.

This approach is among the more popular approaches in conflict management. However, when compromising, you may not always fully resolve the conflict, especially those with complex issues. Sometimes, the needs of one or all the parties are not completely met. This can have drawbacks and retributions if not managed so it's important to assess the risk of compromising when faced with a conflict. Before you create a compromise, gain a comprehensive insight into the needs of the individuals concerned. You will also have to make changes in the project plans.

Compromising is called "give and take" because both parties will have to sacrifice and benefit from the solution to be agreed upon. It's a quick approach that's appropriate for conflicts with time constraints. It's also less confrontational so it will take less effort. However, it's important to make follow-ups after closing the conflict to ensure that no tables are left unturned and the opposing parties don't get lingering feelings of doubt and dissatisfaction about the outcomes.

For example, your team tells you that to complete the initial phase of the project will take four weeks–this includes coordination with partner vendors, procurement, and other preparations. You want it to be completed in two weeks. After a meeting where tasks were delegated, schedules were plotted, timelines were set, and other key responsibilities were aligned, you and the team agreed to close the initial phase within three weeks.

Compromising is best used in situations where:

The needs of both parties must be met.
The negotiation is at a dead end.
The conflict must be resolved immediately.
The relationship between the parties involved are valuable and need to be maintained.
There is little risk in the bargain.

Accommodating. Also known as the smoothing or obligating style, accommodating means highlighting areas of agreement and downplaying areas of disagreement. In other words, accommodating means pacifying the situation by finding the most agreeable resolution. In most cases, one party may have to give way to address the concern of the other or concede to the needs of the other.

Accommodating is your golden ticket to resolving conflict when receding will cause you little to no damage but will be beneficial to the other party involved. This can help in strengthening your connection with other individuals in the situation and maintaining harmonious relationships with other players in your project arena.

When a team is fairly new to a project, accommodating is an effective approach to establish and strengthening group cohesion and relationships. For example, you may easily agree to incorporate recommendations from your team members about improvements in the operational processes, granted that these will not affect critical work path elements.

Another situation where accommodating is appropriate is when you have realized that your position is wrong, and you concede in the conflict. Basically, the accommodating approach works well in putting professional relationships first for the success of the project. However, be wary when using the accommodating approach. Make it a point to reflect when you use this and how you have applied the method.

Being too accommodating can also have a negative effects on your reputation and credibility as a project manager. For others, being too accommodating can put them at risk of being identified as "too willing" or "too soft" and people will constantly take advantage of them.

Competing: Because of its win-lose nature, competing is also referred to as the controlling, forcing, or dominating approach. The competing approach is the opposite of the accommodating approach and is exactly what it sounds—to resolve the conflict; one party strives to win by defeating the other. In this scenario, one person forces his position and pursues his interest despite the resistance of another. The irony, however, is that rather than resolving the conflict, the competing approach intensifies the conflict before arriving at a resolution when it is misused or abused.

Using the competing approach often means enforcing power position to solve the conflict. This is more common among individuals who have a higher authority as compared to the other party in the conflict. Because of this authority, they have the power to influence the situation by issuing a command or imperative.

From time to time, you as the project manager will need to stand your grand and enforce your authority. One of the best scenarios where the use of power is useful is in situations where the risk is high such as emergencies or other situations where the safety of the staff is concerned.

The forcing strategy can also be helpful in a situation where an individual is in a position where he needs to exert dominance through enforcing the power of his authority. For example, a young professional had just been promoted to the level of senior management where most leaders are advanced in age. To prove his competency and make a statement about his authority, he may use the forcing approach in addressing conflict, granted that the risks have been duly calculated, and the decision is well informed.

Competing may also be appropriate when the issue at hand is related to budget or resource matters or when you have the expert knowledge about the matter, which the other party does not. For example, a newly hired employee is presenting a modified scheme in the project plan. He forwards the plan to you and expresses his intent to move the project towards innovation. After a careful review, you note that his proposal, although commendable, is costlier and will require additional and unnecessary work on all stakeholders in the project. While his effort and initiative are appreciated, his proposal is just not feasible at the moment. In this kind of situations, you must put your foot down.

The forcing approach, however, should be used sparingly, especially in your case if you are the leader. If done poorly, forcing can worsen the situation and even cause bigger problems. For one, the opposing party may develop ill feelings toward you. Another scenario could be where the opposing party continues to stand his ground, causing the conflict to escalate and even lead to heated arguments and exchanges.

Forcing or competing does not "resolve" the problem per se; rather, it "squashes" it. However, it allows you to move forward from the conflict, with the risk of compromising positive relationships with the people involved.

The forcing approach is ideal to use when:

The situation calls for a "do or die" measure.
The stakes are high, including valuable principles.
The relationship between the parties is of less importance.
The conflict must be resolved immediately, or a quick resolution is necessary for the conflict.

Avoiding: Avoiding, identified also as the withdrawal style, is an approach were either dealing with the issue is postponed for a later time or the issue is withdrawn completely. When you avoid the conflict, you neither take part in the discussion nor are you helping to resolve it. Avoiding is a temporary solution, not a resolution to the problem.

Because the problem isn't addressed, it doesn't fix the situation and the conflict is bound to surface repeatedly, often it doesn't really solve anything. Although, avoiding isn't necessarily a bad approach. Withdrawing from conflict doesn't mean surrendering. It gives the involved parties' time that can be helpful and beneficial to conflict resolution, especially when the matter is too trivial or too significant.

Dodging a problematic situation where the concern has little to no significance to the project may be necessary. This can give you time to delegate conflict resolution to another individual to focus on more pressing priorities. Avoiding also works well as a self-management technique. It can also reduce the stress for the opposing parties.

When an issue is more complicated, however, it may be beneficial to buy time in resolving the conflict. Some personalities can be prone to outbursts of anger. When you are dealing with this individual, it may be best to use the avoiding approach. It provides the opportunity for the parties involved to calm down and think more clearly and more empathetically, hence, increasing the chance to prepare better to find the best resolution. When you feel that the conflict can be better handled or managed by someone else, such as a third-party mediator from the HR department or an external legal counsel, avoiding is the best approach to use. Avoiding is also appropriate when further investigation is necessary.

As previously mentioned, accommodating is a temporary approach. It provides short-term resolutions to the conflict, so it's imperative that when you apply this style, you must remember to make a follow through—whether it's setting and committing to a reschedule or making a follow up with the third-party mediator assigned.

Be sure to clarify with the parties involved the reason for delaying the mediation and what the following steps will be when you apply the withdrawal approach. Unexplained withdrawals from challenging situations can lead to a loss of respectability as the project leader. Also, it can be viewed by opposing parties as an agreement to their viewpoint.

For example, you have two team members who are engaged in a loud and heated discussion. The commotion has started to disturb others in the area and is causing disruptions in the operation of the project. You can approach them and ask that they pause for a while to cool off. You allow them the time to step out of the office for a short period to get some fresh air and request they return in thirty minutes to discuss the matter in your office.

Another scenario: your client has changed the specifications of the expected output. The new design requires a different set of materials that are more expensive than the original items which have already been accounted for in the budget plans. With some minor revisions in the plan, you accommodated the change request from a client. However, when you presented this to the finance manager, he said there is no longer a way that financial plan can be adjusted. You try to explain that this is a direct request from the client but still the financial manager refuses. Rather than pressing your viewpoint, you thank the financial manager for the time and walk away. Afterward, you gather more data on the feasibility of your proposed plan and present a more comprehensive proposal. Withdrawing from the first discussion with the financial manager allowed you the time to prepare a better presentation to support your ideas. In this scenario, you see that avoiding is just the first step in conflict resolution where you don't really get to solve the problem right away. Resort to another approach to move forward from the conflict.

To know which approach is best to use, it's important to understand the nature of conflict you're dealing with. The first step you will need to take after spotting a red flag is to study the problem and collect as much information as possible. Talk to your people, check your processes and data, and do the ground work to understand the situation. Next, leverage a conflict resolution process. You may also consult with your HR department if they need to be involved. If you don't have an existing conflict resolution process in your organization, you might develop one to be better prepared. Lastly, ensure that you have developed the right culture within your team. A team who is resistant, mistrusting, and wary with each other will be more difficult to mediate and manage during tough times.

One fail-proof technique to use in resolving conflict is active listening. Active listening is necessary for any of the approaches discussed previously. As we mentioned, although there are approaches, which may seem more appropriate or even easier to apply than others may, the context of the conflict should dictate which style is best to use in resolving the problem.

To understand the situation and manage it better, you must actively listen to all parties involved. Active listening means taking the back seat while allowing the conflict to take its natural course. You allow your people to disagree. Let them talk by giving them the avenue to express their opinions no matter how strong. Encourage passionate discourse while keeping the dialogue professional and respectful. Provide minimal input but guide them into realizing on their own criteria acceptable to both parties involved in the conflict.

The key is to foster an open and non-judgmental ambiance where individuals and parties can openly express their needs and interests so you as their leader can gain a good insight into their perspective of the situation. When you as their leader understand their side, there is a better chance you can facilitate the identification of the best approach to resolve the conflict on the ends of the parties. This also strengthens work relationships and creates a culture of trust and respect among your team members.

Set a meeting and lay down ground rules for a safe avenue of discussion. Allow time for each party to present their side or even give a presentation when necessary. Having a formal meeting will help them put their thoughts in perspective and form a structure out of their arguments.

Remember that conflicts are more than what meets the surface. Effective leaders and project managers are on the lookout for underlying problems, not just the symptoms. Therefore, it's important to pay close attention and listen to your people, especially to those involved in the matter. For example, one of your team members has repeatedly exhibited unprofessional behavior toward his coworkers. Repeated incidences that occur despite attempts to coach and correct his behavior may imply deeper causes, such as possible personal problems.

With a solid understanding of the situation, you can then list the advantages and disadvantages of each possible approach to determine how you can best handle the situation. There will be cases, however, where you might feel that the problem is a matter beyond your capability to solve. When this happens, do not panic. It's perfectly normal for professionals to draw their limit and know when to seek help. There are different types of mediators whom you may consider when seeking for assistance to manage conflict:

Asking help from the project sponsor

Delegating the task of managing conflict to a member of your project team, to the HR department, or to a legal counsel

A mediator can be:

The project sponsors
The senior manager or a representative from the senior management team
A neutral member of your project team

A representative from the HR Department
The company's legal counsel

A third-party mediator: A third-party mediator can be a legal counsel hired externally for the purpose of overseeing the management of the conflict. This usually applies to conflicts that are too complex or have legal implications and require the services of a professional. This is a situation you would want to avoid though. Needing the services of an external mediator often means serious problems you would want to do without avoiding jeopardizing your business operations. Also, this means additional cost.

Conflict resolution often requires you to sit down and facilitate conversations with different types of people who may or may not be in a state more difficult to reason with. Because of the accompanying pressure and stress, conflict usually does this to people. This requires you as a project manager and as a leader to have strong interpersonal and communication skills.

It's critical to highlight the importance of being self-aware: knowing how you naturally react in situations where you face opposing opinions and ideas, whether and how much it matters to you if the other party achieves their interests, and how far you are willing to go to win your position. Self-awareness will help you control your personal thoughts and feelings in any difficult situation to maintain objectivism and impartiality when dealing with conflict.

Here are additional practical tips that will help you deal with conflict more effectively:

Set ground rules: At the onset of the project life cycle, define what is within the constraints of acceptable behavior. Encourage healthy professional practices when working interdependently to avoid conflict or to enable your team to manage conflict in a constructive manner.

Ensure that everyone understands their roles and responsibilities and is familiar with the chain of command for effective communication.

Be alert and specific: Because, as mentioned, conflict is like a ticking time bomb. Be vigilant and take conflicts seriously. Once you detect a conflict, at whatever stage it is, be timely in addressing the situation to keep it from escalating into bigger and more complicated problems.

Keep your eyes on the goal: Disagreements often arise because of differing needs and ideas. Remember that in your team, you have one collective goal, which is the success of the project.

Seek to understand the motivations of each person and revert the focus of discussions back to your shared goals to meet at a mutually agreeable decision.

Focus on the facts: It's important to remain objective and logical in any trying situation. Don't allow conflicts to evolve into personal attacks. Focus on the facts and don't jump into any conclusion without seeking to understand all sides of the story to ensure fairness and impartiality in handling the matter.

Focus on the problem, not on the person: Always acknowledge people first and avoid cutting them off when discussing disagreements. This way, you show them that their feelings and ideas are considered and valuable. Don't make conflicts personal and never tolerate attacks towards any person.

Seek to understand first and then seek to be understood. As the project leader, in moments of conflict, your initial goal is to understand all the viewpoints from all parties involved before finding an immediate solution. Make sure people feel they are being listened to. This will leverage your stand when you facilitate and steer the discussion towards finding the best possible solution.

When you have all the information, you can come up with better options and recommendations, which the parties can be more agreeable with because they will see that you have incorporated their ideas into the possible solutions. Then try to explain these clearly and accurately to help them become open to these possibilities.

Choose your battles: Yes, conflicts must be addressed head-on, but this doesn't mean that you must do them yourself. Understand the issue and determine whether the conflict needs to be attended by you directly or can be delegated to someone else, so you can focus on more pressing issues. The role of a project manager has several responsibilities; conflict management is just one among many. Being effective means knowing which tasks need more of your energies and which ones don't.

In conflict resolution, you are not expected to play the role of a therapist or a counselor. As a project manager, your role is to facilitate resolving the conflict as it is. If you find that there are deeper-rooted issues that need to be resolved and are beyond your abilities and scope, don't hesitate to refer the individuals concerned to other professionals who can give them the services they need.

Conflict will surely arise when managing your project whether it involves your team members or you yourself. No amount of planning and risk management can keep differences and disparities from surfacing and leading to disagreements and disputes. However, as we had discussed, conflict can be of significant benefit and is not something you should shy away from.

Look at conflict as a friend and as not an enemy. The best and smartest leaders are constantly looking for windows toward growth–conflicts are just among the many learning opportunities for them and the people they work with. By arming yourself with effective conflict management practices and proactively dealing with them using the correct techniques, seemingly inopportune disputes and disagreements can become positive opportunities for your project and your team.

CHAPTER 9 MANAGING SCOPE

"Let our advance worrying become advance thinking and planning." - Winston Churchill

Projects vary in size and complexity greatly. Some can be short and simple projects while others can be HUGE and require large operations. As the project manager, your task is to ensure that projects stay on track the entire time, no matter how big or complex they are.

Project managers have a responsibility to ensure this because projects are at high risk of failure. Why? A quick search on the reasons projects fail will give you thousands of pieces of literature such as journals, books, blogs and other articles on the many possible reasons. Projects are filled with risk hazards such as incomplete requirements, changing requirements, unclear objectives, inconsistent expectations, and poor management practices.

Looking at all these can seem overwhelming. But the best project managers know the secret on how to keep all these at a minimum to be successful in the pursuit of the project goal: the best way to do this is effective management of the project scope.

What is Project Scope? Project Scope is the output of the initial phase of the development of your project plan. Project scope is the sum of all the elements required in drafting the framework of your project. This includes goals, tasks, features, functions, deadlines, budget, other requirements, and the expected outcome. The scope is the skeleton of your project and the bones of the skeleton are the elements mentioned. When changes on the requirements of the project such as tasks, features, and other requests are created after the planning phase, they are identified as "out of scope" or cause scope change.

Project managers who do not have a strong grasp over the scope of their project are at high risk of being steered by inappropriate, inconsistent, and whimsical ideas, suggestions, and requests from unpredictable, forgetful, or inconsiderate stakeholders. Not that they don't mean well, its common that certain ideas won't reveal themselves until after the planning phase.

It may be difficult for people to describe what it is that they want when a project is still just a theory. Some even suffer from an "I'll know it when I see it" syndrome and provides only a vague idea of what it is they want. And because of the dynamics of personalities, the needs and wants of your stakeholders, your clients, and customers, should be expected to evolve.

Effective scope management involves setting ground rules. Rules your stakeholders can understand and abide by. In addition, this ensures that a project is defined and mapped to enable project managers to allocate all resources necessary to complete the project.

Project scope management includes the process of ensuring that the project includes all the work required to achieve your project goals and the work that is not required as well. Should you fail to define what is and is not part of the project, you and your team are at risk of finding yourself completing work that is unnecessary to meet the main objectives of your project.

Consider a connect the dots puzzle. The dots are arranged and placed in such a way that connecting the dots with lines results in a sequence that will create an illustration of something. What if you missed a dot? What if the order of the dots was misunderstood? The slightest error can ruin the entire picture and give you an image that does not make sense at all. This is like managing the project scope. At the beginning of the implementation of the project, the project requirements need to be laid out in order, similar to the dots. These define the extent to which your project can only go, meaning what should and should not be done. Going beyond the requirements, similar to going beyond the dots, will likely not make it better, instead it will compromise the final output. On paper, the dots in a connect the dots puzzle are not likely to be moved. However, in projects, requirements are not set in stone. Unforeseen changes in scope are likely to happen. And often, it happens through scope creep.

As a project manager, one of your main responsibilities is to manage the defined scope of your project and to meet your stakeholders' expectations. You have to make sure you and your team can carry out and deliver what has been agreed upon in the initial stage of the process cycle.

We've already discussed how change and conflict is a natural phenomenon in the life of a project. Therefore, effective scope management practices should be set in place to prevent the expectations of your project blowing out of proportion and to avoid scope creep.

One illustrative example: your project is to make two liters of tasty, refreshing lemonade. To do this, you were provided with five lemons and a pack of sugar. You and your customer agreed to have the lemonade prepared within half an hour. So you make the drink. Ten minutes later, the customer comes back to you and asks that instead of just two liters you make two and a half. You think it's just half a liter addition; the taste wouldn't change too much. And so, thinking this will not have a significant impact on the work and the resources, you agree. Five minutes later, he comes back and asks if he can have it within the next ten minutes and if you could add another half-liter for a total of three liters. You realize three liters with only five lemons will result in a bland drink. You then request that the client provides additional ingredients. He says requesting for additional budget and purchasing the items will take time. His needs the drinks immediately. Now, this puts you in a difficult position. Because you accepted the initial request and there was no regulation preventing changes, your client expected that you will be able to accommodate his requests and make adjustments with the limited resources you have. What started as a small change request has stretched into an unworkable demand. This is an example of scope creep.

Scope creep is a concept used in the world of project management to identify the phenomenon where projects grow beyond their original and pre-agreed bounds. In other literature, scope creep is also referred to as feature creep, focus creep, creeping functionality, and kitchen-sink syndrome.

If you as project manager do not watch out for scope creep, you may find yourself and your team taking on more work than you had anticipated, and may exceed your available resources, including time and budget. When unmanaged, some changes in the scope of the project can lead to delays in your schedule, stretching of the budget, and other problems. At first glance, this may seem like acceptable and forgivable slip-ups, minor damage that can be solved with a few tweaks in the plan and distribution of resources. However, scope creep, like change and conflict, arises naturally in the project cycle. If ignored and neglected, you could end up disappointing stakeholders or even losing the project altogether.

Scope creep is caused by several factors that can be found in different phases of the project life cycle. For one, poor requirements analysis gives your project plan a weak scope statement, making it difficult to determine which are and are not included in the project scope. Failure to involve stakeholders can also lead to scope creep because of their unmanaged expectations. This can also be credited to poor communication between you, your project team, and stakeholders.

A substandard change control process will also have a significant impact on scope creep. All these will be further discussed in this chapter. It may seem overwhelming because scope change is among the inevitable surprises you will come across in the course of the project life cycle. You can usually expect scope creep to happen. The good news, however, although inevitable, scope creep can be managed and minimized.

So how do we manage scope?

The key is to have a well-defined scope. The scope is the foundation of your project. For example, on a blueprint of a project, everything within the margins of the document is your scope. Having margins on a drawing sheet tells you where you can draw your plan. Your scope will clarify your project objectives and sets the criteria for project completion. As one famous piece of advice goes, begin with the end in mind. Be sure you have a good understanding of the project vision. Setting the scope gives a good picture of the outcome you're expected to deliver upon the completion of the project. However, note that having a defined scope does not put your project in a box. As we discussed in previous chapters, changes in your project are inevitable. The image you had in mind when you begin your project will not be the exact picture of your finished outcome. But as we also discussed, the key to controlling these changes is not to stop but to have effective management practices and mechanisms. This also applies to managing your scope. As you may recall, the idea in managing changes is to ensure that while changes may mean you need to take a different route in our project plan, you still have the same destination—that is to meet our project objectives.

To achieve this, your scope management plan should include the following steps:

Involve key stakeholders
One of the most important yet unwritten roles of a project manager is to serve the key stakeholders of the project and ensure that they are happy and satisfied with the project. To do this, you have to first identify who your stakeholders are. The stakeholders include project sponsors, senior managers, your team members, and support partners, and your clients and customers. It will help you draft a stakeholder's map and see how the connections among these people interplay to know how best to approach them. When you have identified the key stakeholders, you will engage them all throughout the project life cycle, beginning at the planning phase until the project completion.

Don't overestimate your own understanding and make the mistake of thinking you know what the stakeholders want or need without consulting with them first. As you begin to define your scope, start by working out what your stakeholders want from the project. Meet with them and discuss the project overview. Make sure you understand their priorities and that they also understand yours. Perhaps the client wants two sets of the final output done within a six-month period, whereas the current number of the members of your team can only manage to produce one. The senior management will then need to be involved because the client needs to demand an increase in your resources. Here you see how your negotiating skills will also come in handy. As you can see, with the information you've gathered from each one of them, you can integrate their inputs into one large idea, integrate it into your work plan outline, and scope statement.

Write your scope statement
The project scope statement is a summary and consolidation of all the agreements made by the stakeholders. The scope statement should contain what they expect and when they expect it, and what price they will pay for the final output. Make an ordered list of the requirements, including budget, deadlines, features, and metrics of success. Define each deliverable as concurred by the stakeholders. The bigger the project, the more details you should include. Make sure that the scope is clearly defined and communicated to all the parties involved in the project. Go through as many consultations

and revisions as necessary to ensure that they are as accurate and agreeable to all stakeholders. Remember, it's more complicated, time-consuming, and costly to implement changes in the project itself than in the scope statement while it's still in the development phase.

This will be one of your greatest weapons to manage their expectations and to make sure that everyone stays on track with his or her roles and assignments throughout the project life cycle. Having the scope statement will help you avoid constant and unreasonable changes in the project requirements. Also, don't underestimate the complexity of the project.

Many projects can run into problems because of unexplored territories. Be extra careful when venturing in a new industry. When writing your scope statement, be mindful to conduct a risk analysis assessment to identify possible changes and circumstances that can affect the scope later on in the implementation phase. Be sure not to leave any loops open and avoid writing vague statements.

From the previous example, to deliver two sets of the output after six months, you were granted clearance to hire four additional members into the team. The client's request, the expected output within the mentioned time frame, plus the number of people assigned in the project with their specific responsibilities should be well documented and included in the scope statement. This will help you manage client expectations and internal disputes should anyone decide to change their minds.

Breakdown the large idea into smaller chunks of work processes

In this step, you turn back to the listed requirements and translate them into a structured image of what exactly needs to be done. This process will involve your project plan–including tasks, targets, and timelines. The objective is to make work more manageable by breaking them down into smaller chunks. It may be helpful to develop a separate monitoring tool for this. Having a work breakdown chart that's accessible to your team players and other stakeholders will help keep everyone in the project calibrated and at par with what's going on in the project. It may also be helpful to indicate which tasks are assigned to whom.

Scope creep doesn't just happen to the project as a whole, but can affect project team members individually. Changes in the project will also affect the jobs of team members. If changes are left unmanaged and unmonitored, some people might receive additional tasks that were not originally in their terms of reference. In effect, team members might become too burdened and overworked, causing a decrease in morale and productivity. Make sure that in case of scope change, work is evenly distributed and delegated to enable teamwork and maintain fairness among your project team members.

Implement a change request process or a scope change request process. We discussed how to have an effective change management practice. Including implementing a change request process where you and your team have mechanisms to receive process, track, monitor, and evaluate change. This applies just as well to scope management. Create a change request process and educate all your stakeholders about the mechanics of the process. Implement change order forms that are clear and accessible to stakeholders. Have a documentation process for requests coming from your clients and other stakeholders. Conduct a thorough assessment of the change request. Determine the extent of the adjustments necessary to incorporate the change.

As a project manager, it is your responsibility to make sure that changes are aligned with objectives originally agreed upon in the planning phase and is on par with the expected overall outcome agreed on by the stakeholders. Should the change requests be accepted and approved, document how resources and other critical elements will be affected. Communicate immediately to stakeholders and clearly define how the changes will be done and who will be doing them. Check if adjustments need to be made on the schedules and work tasks for your project team members. Update the project plan if needed. Be mindful to evaluate how any change in scope will affect the budget and costing aspects of your projects. Address the process for getting an additional payment for scope changes. Remember that scope change can affect almost every aspect of the project, leading to additional work or rework, thus costing additional time and money. Make sure that stakeholders are aware of this and ensure their accountability for additional costs that the change requests entail.

Ensure that communication is a two-way street

In managing scope change, timely and open communication is critical. Timely meaning quick and efficient, and open meaning transparent, accessible, and engaging. This does not involve only your team, but all stakeholders. Everyone involved, from top to bottom, should be informed of the project.

Having a working knowledge of the scope of the project enables everyone to perform his or her tasks with a clear understanding of what's expected of them and why. However, communication does not stop at delivering and receiving the messages. Communication is most effective when it's a two-way street. The engagement follows effectivity. Encourage your stakeholders to be as open to you. Give them the same respect you wish to be given when communicating the critical elements of the project.

These are just some basic approaches to manage a project effectively. The unpredictable nature of projects makes it trickier to stick a black-and-white strategy. Here are other helpful reminders on how to make sure that your project stays within its original bounds.

Be vigilant from day one. Be careful with your scope, set the right expectations from the beginning of the project life cycle. Change requests may arise as early as the first day of your project. Be clear with the mechanics of change requests and be straightforward in saying yes or no to these requests. Consistency is vital when managing your scope. Hence, be sure to enforce this habit at the beginning of the project until its completion.

Seek to understand your client's needs. To close a project right, start right. Take the time to have a comprehensive understanding of what your client needs and what they expect to get from the project. This will help you map out your project. A thorough dialogue with your client will tell you how urgent the project is, the impact it will make, and the over-all vision your client wants to achieve. With this information, you can assess if the plan is too ambitious and to what extent the plans can further develop.

Be generous with your time and attention for the planning. Never take preparedness for granted. Involve your team in resource planning. Set meetings with adequate time and focus everyone's attention on the objectives. Facilitate risk assessments and resource audits. Ensure that all the requirements are ready once you kick off the implementation of the project.

Cover all your bases when drafting the project scope statement and be careful not to miss any loose ends. Various requirements may have different risks that can't be easily detected at the time of planning.

When conducting risk analysis assessments, it's important to consider how the project may change. Also, be mindful of external factors that can affect your project. Prepare contingency plans in case unexpected circumstances arise. When managing projects, you can never be too prepared.

Clarify the goals and objectives. A well-defined project plan must include a timeline of tasks needed to be accomplished to achieve the project objectives. This is more crucial for bigger projects. It may be helpful to break down tasks into smaller assignments, so you and your team can monitor them properly and avoid scope creep. You might be surprised how a minor change requests can affect your over-all timeline, and resources when left ignored. Take the time to review your progress with your team and balance every development against your timelines to make sure you are still on the same page with your targets. You can find timelines and other tools at: www.wranglingsquirrels.com/resources

Set up a schedule for your deliverables. One of the most effective ways to manage any project is to break down large tasks into smaller sub-tasks and the large-scale work plan into smaller timelines with a focus on the deliverable at the end of each period. This will help you and your team track your progress and develop better accountability in achieving your goals.

Make sure communication lines are always open. Communicating with stakeholders does not end after the planning phase. Scope creep often finds its way into a project when communication lines are not open or somehow blocked. Expectations may not be clearly understood, or certain requirements may be overstretched. Maintaining your baseline is a great way to track your progress and timelines but it is unavailing if it is not communicated properly. Being a project manager also means being a messenger; keep communication lines open.

Prioritize stakeholder feedback. Now, this may seem tricky because one project usually has several stakeholders. If all these stakeholders are providing different inputs all at once, this can create havoc for you and for your team. It's important to place a value on all your stakeholders but be sure to know which ones to prioritize. It's the feedback from the client, which can pivot the project from the original plan. Be sure to manage your backlogs and constantly update the status of each task to see which ones are not along with the critical path elements and which can be delayed to give way to more pressing priorities. This will help you and your stakeholders align and concentrate on matters based on urgency and importance and reduce confusion in the operations of the project.

Consider the timing of scope changes. It's a common understanding among project managers that the further into the project life-cycle a change request is received; the riskier it is in terms of cost, timeline, and work. It's important to conduct an informed appraisal when you receive scope change requests in the middle of the project life cycle. Take into account the work completed and how the change will mitigate your progress. Scope change is less disruptive when it occurs earlier into your timeline. For example, you're in the construction industry and you're currently working on a residential project–a two-bedroom bungalow. Imagine when all arrangements have been made and you and your team have already gone far into installing all the walls when your client suddenly requests to have three bedrooms instead of just two. This change request could have been easier to implement when you were still in the planning phase. Should the stakeholders insist to put into effect these changes, make sure that your stakeholders understand the risks and secure proper documentation on the agreements, especially since there will be modifications and adjustments in the critical elements of your work plan such as cost and timelines.

Keep everyone in the loop, especially your team. A change in scope will often entail some adjustments in your project plan. Make sure to communicate all updates and changes to your project team and concerned stakeholders, especially those who will be directly affected by the changes. Send out official communications to your team and attach necessary documents for their reference. Remember how changes can affect your team, especially when the changes are unexpected and unforeseen. Be mindful to engage them in the change scope process and involve them in decision-making.

Train your team. Watching out for scope creep is not just your sole responsibility. It's critical that your team also have a good understanding of the scope of your project so they not only know what they're supposed to do but also, so they would know when things are going out of bounds. To be able to do this, your team needs to be trained on how to handle changes and act on them.

As project managers, we often have the innate drive to deliver nothing but excellent service for our clients. At times, you might even feel the urge to do more than expected. While this may make your client happy, you must be careful not to over-deliver. Gold plating is a term used to explain the practice of going beyond the scope of the project with the expectation that value is being added. However, this will not only be time-consuming and costlier, but it also does not guarantee customer satisfaction. Moreover, it reinforces the idea that your clients should always expect this kind of service and outcome in future engagements.

Know when to put your foot down. You can expect to receive unreasonable requests on an occasional basis. This is what you get when you work with a variety of personalities who have different needs, demands, and expectations. Do note, however, that not all scope change requests need to be accepted. Changes that will have a major impact on the critical elements of the project such as a timeline and budget need to be scrutinized with the utmost care. If the scope change request will hold up a significant part of the work and cause a delay in your schedule, make a well-informed decision whether to accommodate the request. As the project manager, you control the traffic light in these kinds of situations: you get to say which gets green-lighted (approved), red-lighted (rejected), or even yellow-lighted (delayed for further review or scheduled for a later period).

If saying no is non-negotiable, find a different bargain to make ends meet. In situations where you are not in the position to say no (such as when your senior manager authorizes the request), you can consider other alternatives:

- When scope change brings new items to your work plan, analyze which items can be removed or cut.

- When scope change requests need to be attended to but are not urgent, you can give them the yellow-light by developing a backlog or a sub-project you can delay.

Match the scope changes with a price. Test how much is the additional cost for additional features in the output. Remember, add attributes to any product or service also means an increase in the revenue.

One important thing to note when talking about scope is a stakeholder's perception of the value of a project, its deliverable, management processes, and the manager itself. How you manage scope will ultimately influence this perception. The value is determined by the expectations of the stakeholders versus the reality of the actual delivered product. When the delivered product does not meet the expectations, stakeholders perceive the project to be of less value. If the project outcomes meet or even exceed the expectations, stakeholders will have a positive value perception, which in effect means happy stakeholders and satisfied clients and customers. Considering all the scope management practices to be aimed towards achieving a positive value perception.

It's easy to want to rush through planning as quickly as possible to get started on doing the actual work. The idea is to deliver results with as much efficiency as possible. To make your clients and customers happy. Project teams can get too excited to get down to the good stuff and see the plan come to life. However, rushing through the critical steps of gathering the relevant information from your stakeholders, defining a clear and compliant scope, and outlining the project will put you at great risk of contending with the pains of unruly scope creep in due course. Although changes in scope should well be expected in any project, its inevitability does not make it unmanageable. Through effective scope management practices, you can keep changes in scope to a minimum. While we have discussed several approaches you can apply, there are more things you can do. The key is to find the strategies that best suit your strength, that is amenable to your stakeholders, and that is appropriate in the context of your project. Remember, what you want to achieve is to move forward in the project with as little disruption as possible.

CHAPTER 10 MEASURING PROGRESS, SUCCESS, AND FAILURE

"One of the true tests of leadership is the ability to recognize a problem before it becomes an emergency." -Arnold Glasow

In the last nine chapters, we've talked about how to be an effective project manager. We've inspected some of the most common project management concepts from a less-common perspective, and identified practical strategies that you can use to carry out a project. All the fundamental abstractions of project management, however, would be in vain if we don't know if our efforts are making a difference. We've talked about understanding project objectives, aiming to meet target goals, and even pulling the plug on projects when we foresee that they're bound to fail. This leads us to the final question we will seek to answer in this book. Tracking progress: how do we measure success and failure?

A project manager may have a good grasp on everything else, but if they don't know how to tell if they are heading toward success, all efforts may be in vain. How do we then define success? Is it when a client signs off on the project? Is it when funding has been approved? Is it when each major milestone achieved? Is it when work is completed?

All formally educated/trained project managers know the basic concept of monitoring and evaluation. They often involve focused approaches. Some project teams even have a designated Monitoring and Evaluation Officer solely dedicated to this purpose. This isn't always the case, however. The presence of a Monitoring and Evaluation Officer depends on the availability of resources. It's expected that measuring project success is also on the list of your responsibilities as a project manager–even when you have a Monitoring and Evaluation Officer. With everything going on in the project life cycle and the amount of work you're putting into the project, you want to make sure you and your team are on the right track, and what you're doing is achieving the results you're aiming for.

Often, a project has not just a few, but several indicators of success. It can get tricky for project managers to determine how much time exactly to spend evaluating past performance and how much time exactly to spend on keeping the wheels of the project moving forward. Project monitoring and evaluation means ensuring that you can keep an eye on how the project is performing against the project work plan and the scope statement. Remember that your scope builds the framework of what you want to achieve upon completing the project. To get a real measure of the success of a project, you need to check if the results have met the objectives from its given framework, which is the scope.

But what exactly do we need to measure? Far too often project teams begin the implementation phase without defined success criteria. Either that or they begin with the wrong set of criteria. In this chapter, we'll talk about the factors you should measure to gauge the success of a project. We will go beyond the traditional business requirements and consider the project success criteria that you must identify and document in order to know if you're hitting the marks in your project.

The success criteria are the identified standards by which your project will be judged. These will serve as your indicators to determine if the project is successful. Project success criteria are very important. It integrates everything else we've discussed so far. In most cases, organizations do not define failure. Yes, there are specific key performance indicators that are provided and need to be met, however, it is uncommon for organizations to talk about failing because it does not provide effective motivation. Unfortunately, the absence of defining failure makes it difficult for the project manager and project teams to know if the course of the project implementation is still on the right path or not. Therefore, even if it might not always be comfortable, especially for new projects and teams, effective project managers take necessary steps to ensure that project success is clearly defined by the project success criteria.

As we are discussing project management concepts that are more practical and realistic, let's state another unpopular fact: projects are as likely to fail as they are to succeed. To better understand the value of success, we must know the pains of failure.

Here are some reason's projects fail:

- Lack of visibility. All roles involved in the project, namely the executive team, project managers, and the project teams, need to have access to the right level of information at the right time. In most fast-paced environments, project managers and executive teams often handle more than one project at a time. So, a work plan and schedule is crucial, not just to be drafted but to be updated and communicated regularly.

- Unclear project objectives. Organizations and project teams often have more project opportunities and more project initiatives than they can fulfill and deliver. Poor planning and prioritization lead to unclear project objectives, jeopardizing project outcomes and overall performance.

- Communication gaps. You may notice how it has been repeated throughout this book that communication is key. One simple way to illustrate a communication gap that can harm your chances of project success is your dependence on using email for communication. Almost all, if not all, project managers rely heavily on using emails to communicate with the project teams about updates on the project. The problem is when emails get stuck or lost in in-boxes because of the excessive volume of mail received, or when someone forgets to click on Reply to All and everyone else is left in the dark with further updates.

- Incomplete tools and training. You can have the best roster of members in your team but still will not be able to perform successfully if they don't have the necessary tools. Also, with the highly dynamic trends in the industry, it's imperative that their competencies and skills are being continuously developed with training and knowledge-building activities.

- Poor risk management. Regular tracking and monitoring enable you as a project manager to keep an eye on your process flow. Through this, you will catch potential problems as early as possible to make timely adjustments to the project, so it can continue running smoothly with fewer mistakes.

What should we be on the look-out for then to make sure we know if our project is heading in the right direction? Throughout the project life-cycle, you should be evaluating the following points:

SCHEDULE
The success of your project is largely determined by whether you and your team were able to work within the original timeline that was agreed on by the stakeholders. Even the slightest delay can cause a huge dent on your reputation and credibility in the industry of project management. Despite all these potential issues, you must be able to complete the project by the time it is due. You want to ensure that you will be known for working efficiently and delivering on time–always. Though the experience will tell you that keeping a schedule is not as simple as it seems, careful and consistent monitoring of your progress as you go along the project life cycle will help you achieve this.

Your team's schedule, both collective and individual, should be updated regularly, at least every week. A formal evaluation of your project schedules must be conducted on a monthly basis. If possible, gather your team and have a formal sit-down with them to discuss where each one is at the project life cycle. Look into your major milestones and check if they fall on the same dates as you had originally planned to achieve them. Analyze each one's progress and the team's collective movement. Compare this rate with your original timelines. If you observe discrepancies (slippages and delays), explore the possible impact these will have on your overall timeline. Discuss what measures are necessary to bring everyone back on the right track.

Document these discussions and furnish a copy to your team members. Remember, communication is key. Regular evaluations are worth nothing if not communicated. Ensure that your stakeholders are informed of the results of these discussions. Present a regular monthly report on your progress, showing at what phase or stage you are at in the project. Some clients are strict with deadlines whereas you may encounter some who are only interested in the final product. As a project manager, it builds up your credibility by working with a schedule you are always aiming to meet.

QUALITY
There's a general belief that quality check applies only for the output of a project–whether it's a product or a service. Quality reviews are important in determining if your project is a success or a failure because it tells you if

the tasks your team is doing is meeting the standards set out in project requirements, specifically in terms of quality. However, the quality review can apply to the project management practices as well. This includes the implementation of the change management process, conflict management, business negotiations, and even stakeholders' perspective management. Your goal in conducting quality reviews should not focus solely on the deliverable's but also on the evaluation of whether your current project management practices are meeting the project requirements according to the original work plan and quality requirements.

COST

Perhaps one of the most, if not the most, crucial priorities in handling projects is cost management. The financial performance of the project will ultimately determine the fate of the project. Did you and your team stick to the budget? Did you come in under budget? Spend too little, you compromise the quality of your performance and output. Spend too much, you compromise the critical elements of the project execution. Therefore, it takes a keen eye for finances and a reasonable skill set in financial literacy and management to be a truly effective project manager. You and your team should always be aware of where you stand in terms of money spent and available. Remember that poorly managed change requests and uncontrolled scope creep can have a negative impact on your budget. Having a work plan with a clear-cut financial scheme does not guarantee your security in budget allocation and expenses. In addition to calibrating work schedules and job progress, it's also important to set official consultations with your team to check actual expenditures and compare them to the initial budget plan. Variances in transactions should be explained and justified in accordance with the business case.

Because money is a paramount factor in this role (it can literally make or break you and the project), it will be in your best interest to conduct several reviews. Re-forecast the budget plan as needed to see how the scheme may be affected through the end of the project life cycle. Conduct a recurring comprehensive risk assessment and allot contingency funds for allowances. This will be helpful for you and your team in case of change requests that need additional funding. Always look back to your original budget plan to be well-informed if you and your team is going out of bounds with the allowable changes in your budgeting and expenditures. If your assessments tell you that the current processes will require you to spend beyond your means, call for a time-out and reassess your strategies. You can find simple Budget Plan templates and ideas at: www.wranglingsquirrels.com/resources

In the world of project management, your aim is to stick to your budget and come in under when possible. Remember, you want to aim for profitability, not just compliance.

PRODUCTIVITY

Productivity is determined by the number of outputs produced per unit of input invested in the project. In other words, Productivity will help determine if your stakeholders are getting their money's worth from the project and your project team. Productivity, however, can vary across different projects and their requirements. Other productivity metrics include the number of projects completed per employee, the number of outputs produced within a specific period, etc. To identify the correct way to measure productivity for a certain project, consider your stakeholders and the value they place on the output being measured. This is also directly related to the next success criteria.

STAKEHOLDER AND TEAM SATISFACTION

The project stakeholders, who are not part of your project team members, are still team members that make up the outer circle. You can't expect them to be the most cooperative, but they play a significant role in bagging a win for your project. An unwritten responsibility of being a project manager is to make sure that your stakeholders are "happy" with the project and pleased with the outcomes. The timelines may have been met, you might not have gone over your budget, the quality of work may be as fine, but if your stakeholders are displeased you'll still be missing the mark to be successful in the project.

What makes satisfaction more difficult to manage than the other indicators of success is that there is no objective and standardized way to measure it. Satisfaction is highly subjective and can change without warning. It is hard to forecast and control, but it's not impossible. Remember, in the previous chapter where we discussed how it is difficult for people to clearly identify and explain what they want from a project? The stakeholders put a human touch to the monitoring and evaluation of projects. It's a challenging yet useful exercise to make subjective calculations on how your stakeholders feel about the performance of the project team and the project itself. It's also a part of the responsibility of the project manager to understand their needs and make sure they're happy with the outcome. Get their constant feedback to avoid any misunderstanding and oversight. If you notice that your stakeholders are rather reserved or unsupportive, you can create your own action plan on how to build good work relationships with them and engage them meaningfully to influence their behavior and attitudes. Even if they are the outer circle of your crew, you need your stakeholders to be present, committed, and on your side.

Customer satisfaction, or end to end-user reception is a vital criterion. Customer satisfaction means that customer expectations are met. Another success criterion is team satisfaction. Though under the same category, team satisfaction is a less popular success indicator, but how successful can a project really be if the team isn't happy? Often, project teams are taken for granted, because there are more pressing priorities. when it comes to project management, some might say it's what they're supposed to do. However, a happy workplace is a more productive workplace and a happy workplace is more likely to produce successful outcomes and deliver results.

One of the simplest ways to gauge satisfaction is to ask all the parties involved or at least a representative of each party. Questions can be as straightforward as: Were you satisfied with the outcomes? Were you happy during the implementation? If not, this indicates that there were inefficiencies in the project. In this situation, don't hesitate to probe further. Ask the stakeholders for their recommendations on what could be improved. Ask your project team members which processes or techniques they feel can be strengthened or if changes are necessary to increase future satisfaction ratings.

PERFORMANCE AGAINST BUSINESS CASE

One final success indicator that's often overlooked is the business case. The business case is given due attention at the time of planning. However, it also pays to check regularly how the project is shaping up comparing it to the business case. Is the project advancing into something that is still realistic? Something still timely? Something still relevant? Did it meet the needs of the end users? Engage with your stakeholders by asking them: Did the results of the project benefit the business and the parties involved? What other benefits would they like to see from future projects? A general aim of almost all projects is to realize the benefits for its stakeholders. If the project was completed but was not able to produce worthwhile or noticeable benefits, you may have to carefully review the project objectives and ensure that future project objectives will lead to beneficial outcomes for your stakeholders.

There are other success metrics you can consider, depending on the requirement of the project. Some possible metrics include:

Return of investment
Return on expectation
Competitive advantage
Opportunities identified
Process improvements
Refined reporting procedures
User empowerment

When establishing your success criteria, be mindful to take into consideration the following:

Your success criteria should be aligned with the original business requirements agreed upon during the planning phase of the project life-cycle. Review the original project documents to ensure that the metrics and numbers you and your team are monitoring are on par with the business requirements – whether it concerns the deliverables or the process.

Prioritize:
We have discussed a number of factors that can be identified as the determinants of project success. While all of these are important and have a significant bearing in the achievement of a project's success, project managers must know how to prioritize. It is important to consider the factors that are critical to the project, based on the project goals, the business requirements, and the expectations of the clients and other stakeholders. Some projects require more attention for deliverables, whereas some projects might have higher stakes on the process itself. There are other projects that place the highest on the return of investment.

Attainability:
As with all project management goals, your success criteria must be realistic and attainable. Don't set impractical and unreasonable targets for your project and your team as this can add unnecessary pressure and stress.

Precision and quantifiability:
With certain exceptions to the stakeholders' satisfaction criteria, project success criteria should be accurate and measurable. It's also essential to know how these criteria will be measured and monitored. On top of all the hustle

and bustle in running your project, you don't want to confuse your team in the monitoring of your progress. Try to make the evaluation process as simple and concise as possible, with a clear-cut formula or process that's easy for everyone involved to understand. Remember, if the project you're undertaking cannot be measured, there's not much point in pursuing it. Projects should have objectives and goals that are clear, precise, and measurable.

Change in scope and requirements:
You can expect your project plan to evolve as the project life cycle progresses. Because of this, you must ensure that your success criteria follow the same pace with these changes.

When managed and presented properly, these measures of success can serve as your team's scoreboard – this can help you and your team stay on track and set a rallying point for everyone involved in the project.

The next question is how do we measure these indicators and how do we check if we're hitting the targets? Depending on the project, the implementation, the expected deliverables, and the stakeholders themselves, a monitoring strategy should ideally, include:

Getting your team involved:
Collaboration is one of your best weapons. Your project team is a highly valuable resource for the success of a project. From the beginning, cultivate an ambiance of teamwork and unity and engage with them regularly even after they move forward with their own unique responsibilities under the project. When deciding on the project success criteria, the definition, standards of measurement, expected measure output, and assignment of responsibilities, provide them an avenue to provide their input and recommendation. Make sure that each person is trained to carry out the monitoring and evaluation mechanisms and schedule a regular check-in with your team where you can discuss progress updates and determines areas of improvements. Begin and continuously move forward with the end in mind. The project goal serves as the anchor for you and your team. Constant visualization of the end goal increases the chance of translating it into reality. In tracking your progress, having an end in sight from the beginning will give a benchmark for decision-making and other actions concerning the project.

Implement and use project monitoring tools:

There are hundreds of tools that project managers can choose from to help them in measuring the progress of their projects. A few categories of these tools include: Gantt Chart, Visual Maps, Timetables and Project Dashboards. These are often easy to use and provides you and your team the convenience of having a visual representation of your progress as you move towards completion.

Plot your milestones:
Continuing with the analogy we made early in this chapter, the project milestones are the dots in your connect-the-dots puzzle. Each milestone indicates a beginning and an end of major phases in your project. They should be completed sequentially. If not, you'll come up with a distorted output. Milestones are complementary to your work breakdown structure. It schedules your project into smaller, digestible parts and helps measure your progress on a large scale. The work breakdown structure is a highly useful tool as it presents the different milestones that need to be accomplished over a measured amount of time. This will help you in distributing tasks, managing change requests, ensuring scope completion and monitoring the progress of the project implementation.

Set deadlines:
Deadlines give a sense of urgency. It'll be one of your major drivers in getting things done efficiently. Compared to working with an open schedule, having a deadline will prevent delays and it will also give you and your team markers across the project schedule.

Provide recommendations for improvement and follow-up:
This is among the primary objectives of monitoring and evaluation: to provide recommendations for corrective actions, preventative actions, or other necessary changes in the project plan or processes. There is always room for improvement, no matter how smooth-sailing a project life cycle is. As a project manager, it's also your job to look over the data gathered in your monitoring and evaluation process to find these areas of improvement. This can be directed toward the entire project team or to just one individual. This can also be an opportunity for coaching and skill enhancement. With these inputs, use follow-ups to confirm that recommendations and changes are being implemented. Continue monitoring the team's collective progress to ensure that expected outputs are being delivered and that the project team is on track.

Consider these other steps as well:

Conduct a project meeting with stakeholders weekly or monthly, depending on the project duration

Conduct project audits according to the work plan schedules

Conduct regular project quality reviews based on the project scope requirements

There are two ways to estimate the success rate of a project:

One is through discrete measures. The discrete evaluation is done by asking questions that are answerable by either yes or no. This is generally focused on whether something has been or has not been done. For example, did we meet the deadline for this task? Did we produce six hundred units of the output? Did we open the new branch in time for the launch? Were we granted the business accreditation? Did we meet our sales quota for this month? While we will be able to determine if a certain target is achieved, discrete measures will not provide us the information as to what extent it was attained.

The other type of measure is called continuous measurement. The continuous measurement involves assessing if something has been done a certain extent within a specific target range. For example, were we able to increase customer satisfaction survey scores from 70% to 90% within a two-month period? Were we able to recruit 50 more customers taking part in our 3 branches within the last quarter?

Both measures can determine whether you have achieved the criteria or not. In fact, continuous measures are also always counted as discrete evaluations, but with more specific and quantifiable information. If the customer satisfaction scores increased from 70% to 90%, then we can say, yes, we improved the satisfaction surveys by 20% in two months. However, a discrete measure will limit your analysis of your progress. Saying, yes, there is an increase, will not tell us how large the increase was or what is the difference of the scores from those two months and the period before that. Another example is when you are measuring success regarding work schedules. Were you able to hit all of your milestones on time? If not, how far behind the schedule was it? If not, at what rate do you need to increase your pace on the current task to still meet your overall deadline? If you want to produce information which you can use to compare your performance or the quality of your outputs, go for continuous measurements whenever you can. This will also be useful for future evaluation of possible opportunities for business and process improvements.

Other tips:
Collect timely and relevant data. After having identified the success criteria for a specific project, define each metric and show the kind of data needed to represent each criterion. Remember that this data should help you and your team define the project's successes and failures, and will be used as references to identify necessary action plans to help strengthen the project or to be developed as knowledge for future projects and undertakings.

Time is the key factor. Besides ensuring that the data you gather for your success metrics are timely, it's also critical that you monitor your success over a specific and relevant time period. Monitoring should not be done at just one point in the project life cycle. The success criteria should be measured during and after the execution of the project, so you can get a clear and complete picture of your progress.

Engage your stakeholders. Project success criteria are not just useful for monitoring and evaluation but are also helpful in generating engagements with your stakeholders. As we mentioned earlier, communication is crucial to the success of your project. Implement an internal communication strategy to keep your stakeholders in the loop regarding your progress. Through these engagements, you will also be able to determine if your stakeholders are losing interest in the project. In such a case, consider this as an early warning sign you need to exert more effort to keep them on your side.

Ask how you can help. Talking about due dates, milestones and targets can be stressful for project team members. As a project manager can help them feel less threatened and pressured by providing your support in several ways. One is to suggest additional tools that are available to help them with organization skills. Another could be additional coaching and implementing a buddy system for review that can help your project teams during times of excessive workload. It's also important to be available for your project team members and keeping communication lines open.

Prioritize, prioritize, prioritize. As a project manager, remember that it's critical that you manage your time. Set your focus on the most important things. Remember, you can only do so much and you cannot track everything. Decide on which project success criteria is most crucial. It will be beneficial to you and your team members to delegate effectively.

On a final note, don't take for granted the value of documenting the identified success criteria. List them out in an organized and presentable fashion that's easy to refer to and easily understood by your stakeholders. At minimum, include these items in the list items: (1) Name of success criteria, (2) Standard of measurements, (3) Frequency and schedule of measurements, (4) Person/s responsible for that specific success criteria, and (5) Output of the specific measure. Having documented success criteria means you can get your stakeholders to concur and sign on them. This helps with your scope management. Should project and scope changes happen, don't forget to update your success criteria as well.

Monitoring and evaluation integrates pretty much everything we talked about in the past several chapters–monitoring: (1) your team and the people you work with, (2) relationships or partnerships with other entities involved in the project, (3) changes in scope and other project elements, (4) critical project requirements, and (5) yourself as project manager.

There are hundreds of things that can impede the project goals and the successful completion of a project. With so many things going on related to budgeting, schedules, labor distribution, group dynamics and business relationships to name a few, it's easy to get so lost in the process of making sure everything is working smoothly that you forget to check if everything is working towards success. Be mindful and take a moment to place yourself outside of the project itself and look at it from a wider perspective–not just to see if things are going according to plan but if the plan itself is working. You want to have a bird's-eye view to ensure that you and your project team are on target in the eyes of your stakeholders, clients and customers, and on track with your project requirements. This way you'll know not only how far along you are working towards your project goals, but also how far you've gone from the beginning of project execution.

Again, when managing projects, you want not just to complete a project, but also to complete a project that has made your stakeholders happy.

CHAPTER 11 Goals

"First, have a definite, clear practical ideal; a goal, an objective. Second, have the necessary means to achieve your ends; wisdom, money, materials, and methods. Third, adjust all your means to that end."
- Aristotle

Project management is not easy; whether you're a seasoned project manager or new to the field, the job is going to be stressful regardless of how many times you experience it. But the rewards – every successful project, every victorious team, every accomplished goal – will be worth every effort. The best project managers put their faith in the process and learn from their struggles.

The project management concepts and resources covered in this book provide a broad scope of competencies that will help you prepare for the life of a project manager and strengthen your reputation as an effective leader. As we've discussed in the previous chapters, you will face different scenarios, some of which will require you to communicate with different personalities, make on-the-spot decisions, adapt to unforeseen changes in your plan or make and break relationships.

Set your goals and be very clear with what you want to achieve in your project. This will serve as your anchor when the going gets tough. Make sure every decision and action you take is directed towards your goals. The success of any project is determined by the people who work together to achieve the project's common goal. The right team is motivated, committed, and empowered. Find people whom you believe you can trust and whose passion, abilities and capabilities are aligned with the goals of the project. As their leader, you have to constantly see that they share the same vision, so that when your project hits a bump and things become challenging, you won't have to worry too much about their ability to cope.

Your senior leaders will play a major role in getting your project to where you want it to be, but this doesn't mean that you can't have a hand in steering the wheel in the direction that you want to go. The key is to build meaningful relationships with your team, your leaders, and other stakeholders. Maximize your role as project manager and as a leader and manage not only downward but upward to make the most out of your position and set up your project and your team for success.

The best project managers always approach every situation with a win-win objective. They are not self-serving nor egocentric. Their best interest is with the success of the project and their teams. Effective project managers know how to strike the balance between being idealistic and realistic. They put their team on the pedestal for their individual professional development and they recognize productivity and positive performance. A successful leader paves the way for his people to grow into leaders as well. He sees their potential and enables them to realize their capabilities by providing them opportunities through delegation of tasks and fair distribution of work among them.

Build your team up and help them appreciate the concept of dynamism. Train them to understand that a project plan is ever-changing but your goals towards success are not. Help them acknowledge that change is inevitable, but growth is a choice. The best project managers are visionaries who see opportunities in changes rather than challenges. They know to find the best solutions that will lead them to the common ground where the best outcomes will benefit not just them, but everyone involved in the undertaking as well. Build your team up and help them appreciate the concept of dynamism. Train them to understand that a project plan is ever-changing but your goals towards success are not. Help them acknowledge that change is inevitable, but growth is a choice. The best project managers are visionaries who see opportunities in changes rather than challenges. They know to find the best solutions that will lead them to the common ground where the best outcomes will benefit not just them, but everyone involved in the undertaking as well.

Beyond the theoretical knowledge, equipping yourself with these practical skills will help you become a more effective project manager. So now that you've come to the end of the final chapter, put this book down, get up and put what you've learned to practical use. The best teacher is experience and there are a lot of squirrels waiting for you to take them on.

Printed in Great Britain
by Amazon